CORNERSTONES
of the RESTORATION

CORNERSTONES
of the RESTORATION

M. GARFIELD COOK

❄

Salt Lake City, Utah

First printing: Fall 1998
Revised edition: Spring 1999

Library of Congress Cataloging-in-Publication Data

Cook, M. Garfield, 1940-
    Cornerstones of the Restoration / by M. Garfield Cook.
        p. cm.
    Includes index.
    ISBN 1-56713325-8
    1. Gospel symbolism.   2. Calculation of dates in religious
history.
I. Title
98-73936
  CIP

Printed in the United States of America
by
Hiller Book Binders
631 North 400 West
Salt Lake City, Utah 84103

10 9 8 7 6 5 4 3 2

Table of Contents

Preface

The writing of this small volume of study began at three a.m. on Mother's Day 1996. Sleep fled as a strong impression came over me that the dates of key events pertaining to the restoration of the kingdom of God were set in the *cornerstones* of the restored Church noted by President Gordon B. Hinckley, namely, Jesus Christ (the Chief Cornerstone), the First Vision, the Book of Mormon, and the Apostles and Prophets (*Ensign*, Nov. 1984, pp. 50-52). Isaiah said:

> Thus saith the Lord God...I lay in Zion for a foundation a stone, a tried stone, a precious corner *stone*, a sure foundation...Judgment also will I lay to the line, and righteousness to the plummet" (Is. 28:16-17).

I reflected again and again on this "precious cornerstone" and on the gospel symbolism associated with it; and I assumed that if numerical dimensions were to be assigned to a geometric symbol representing this cornerstone, they would be found in the numerical parameters of Jesus' life and ministry.

The scriptures tell us that after the Fall "the Almighty God gave his Only Begotten Son" and gave commandments that all mankind "should love and serve him, the only living and true God, and that he should be the only being whom they should worship" (D&C 20:19, 21). "All things which have been given of God from the beginning of the world, unto man, are the typifying" of Jesus Christ (2 Ne. 11:4).

So at three a.m. on Mother's Day 1996, I set out to discover from scripture what such a cornerstone might look like diagrammatically and what information it might contain. I assumed that a chief cornerstone symbol would contain information relating to Joseph Smith and the First Vision, and to the restoration of the Book of Mormon, the Priesthood, and the kingdom of God. But of surprise to me was the fact that it seemed to be the foundation of a tree of life symbol which, when defined by numerical parameters from Jesus' life and ministry, contains information regarding specific dates of key events relating to those subjects. Furthermore, the English rendering of the Jehovah (YHWH) and the Alpha (Λ) and Omega (Ω) signs could also be seen in a combined chief cornerstone and tree of life symbol when so defined.

We live in the dispensation which "our forefathers have awaited with anxious expectation,...which their minds were pointed to by the angels, as held in reserve for the fulness of their glory" (D&C 121:27). This is the dispensation of the fulness of times, about which the Lord said: "I will gather together in one all things, both which are in heaven, and which are on earth;... Wherefore, lift up your hearts and rejoice..." (D&C 27:13, 15). The truths flowing from the restoration of the kingdom of God are like a well of *living waters* which never cease, of which a person may drink and never thirst again (John 4:14; 1 Ne. 11:25).

I dedicate this book to the mother of my nine children, my dear wife, Margo, whose love, patience and devotion are greatly appreciated, and to our mothers, Wanda, and JoAnn.

—M. Garfield Cook
Spring 1999

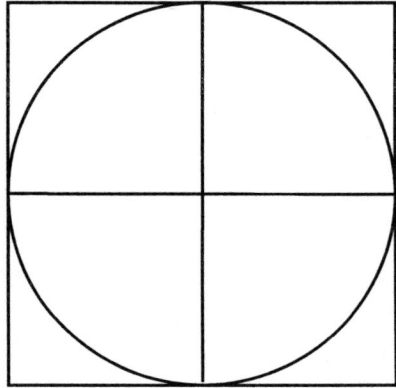

Key Dates of the Restoration

1805 —23 December. Joseph Smith was born in Sharon, Windsor County, Vermont. (Equations 1 and 1.1)

1820 —(26 March calculated). The Father and the Son appeared to Joseph Smith in what has since been called "The First Vision." (Equation 2)

1823 —21-22 September. Joseph Smith received the first visit from the Angel Moroni who revealed the existence and location of the Book of Mormon plates which contain the fulness of the gospel of Jesus Christ. (Equations 3 and 3.1)

1827 —22 September. Joseph Smith received the Book of Mormon plates from Moroni. (Equation 4)

1829 —15 May. Joseph Smith and Oliver Cowdery received the Aaronic Priesthood from John the Baptist. (Equation 5)

1829 —(28 May calculated). Joseph Smith and Oliver Cowdery received the Melchizedek Priesthood from Peter, James, and John. (Equation 6)

1830 —6 April. The Church of Jesus Christ of Latter-day Saints was organized. (Equation 7)

1836 —3 April. The Son of Man, Moses, Elias and Elijah appeared to Joseph Smith and Oliver Cowdery in the Kirtland Temple. (Equation 8)

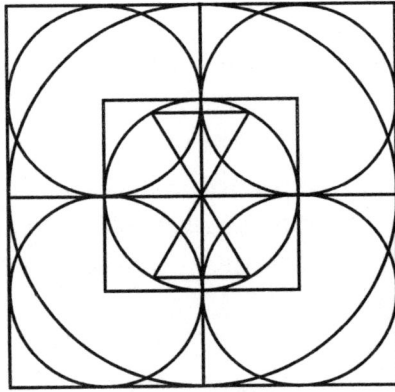

Chapter 1

A MESSAGE EXTRACTED
FROM A GENEALOGICAL RECORD

> "So all the generations from Abraham to David
> are fourteen generations; and from David until
> the carrying away into Babylon are fourteen
> generations; and from the carrying away into
> Babylon until Christ are fourteen generations"
> (Matt. 1:17).

The New Testament begins with a genealogical record of Jesus the Christ. Matthew says that there were 42 generations from Abraham to Christ. The King James Version presents these generations in fifteen verses with one summary verse. The Joseph Smith Translation presents them in three verses with one summary verse (JST Matt. 1:2-5). This highlights the 3 x 14 aspect of these 42 generations and suggests that an important message is thereby being conveyed. The *Chief Cornerstone* of the kingdom of God (Is. 28:16; Eph. 2:20) provides the basis for extracting this genealogical message.

Symbols and Numbers
Symbols are the universal language God has used to reveal gospel ordinances and covenants. Symbols help us remember them and the teachings associated with them. Geometric forms and patterns are often used to present messages. A square, for instance, conveys the idea of exactness, integrity, and moral rectitude. It may also be used as a symbol for the earth in its four corners or quarters. A circle symbolizes eternity and may be used to represent the course of God, namely, one eternal round (D&C 3:2).

Jesus taught in parables and in symbols. Orson F. Whitney said: "God teaches with symbols; it is his favorite way of teaching" (*Improvement Era*, Aug. 1927, p. 851). "All things have their likeness" and "all things" were created and made to bear record of Jesus Christ. This is true of things both temporal and spiritual, "things which are in the heaven above, and things which are on the earth" beneath (Moses 6:63).

Numbers may also be used to convey messages, either by themselves,[1] or by adding, subtracting, dividing, or multiplying them as in the 3 x 14 example above. They may be raised to a power to emphasize a message and/or to indicate the number of concepts being presented. When the same symbolic number is used with different units of measure, a correlation is implied between the two messages being conveyed. When numerical parameters from Jesus' life and ministry are used as dimensions for *geometric* forms, it can be shown that dates of key events in the restoration of the latter-day kingdom of God *on earth* have been set forever in *geometric* form. For instance, it can be shown that Joseph Smith's birth year was set in the squared circle.

The Godhead consists of the Father, the Son, and the Holy Ghost (D&C 130:22). The numbers 1, 2, and 3 might be used in reference to them, respectively. The number 3 may also represent spirit, or the power of God, or the light which proceeds forth from his presence—the light which is in all things and is the law by which all things are governed" (D&C 88:12-13).

---

[1]Smith's Bible Dictionary, "Number".

The number 4 references the *whole earth*. The number 12 squared $(4 \times 3)^2$ emphasizes the *worldwide testimony* of 12 Apostles of the Firstborn (1 Ne. 1:10) and of 12 Tribes of Israel that are compared to the Firstborn (Ex. 4:22). The number 1000 (10^3) emphasizes the *omnipotence, omniscience, and omnipresence* of God relative to mortal man (2 Pet. 3:8; 1 Jn. 2:20, 27). Multiplying 12^2 by 1000 bespeaks the *divine power* that 144,000 high priests, who are ordained out of *every nation, kindred, tongue, and people*, will have over the nations of the *whole earth* to bring as many as will come to the Church of the Firstborn (Rev. 7:4; D&C 77:11).

Units of Measure
The same number used with different units of measure is a powerful teaching device. It was used to teach the age of accountability. Abraham was given a law that male children should be circumcised when 8 *days* old so that his *seed* (p. 8) would remember that children are not accountable until they are 8 *years* old (JST Gen. 17:11). Peter noted that in Noah's Ark "8 *souls* were saved by water" (1 Pet. 3:20). Alma used 8 *elements* to teach the baptismal covenant (Mosiah 18:8-10). It was 8 *days* after the ascension that 3 x 1000 *souls* were baptized (Acts 2:41). The companionship of the Holy Ghost 3 x 8 *hours per day* follows obedience to the baptismal covenant (Moro. 8:25-26; D&C 121:46). Through baptism the *Truth* submitted himself to the Father (½) and truth shines from the Sun to earth in 8 and ½ *minutes* (John 14:6; D&C 88:7, 11). A musical octave is consonant. Baptism symbolizes rebirth (Rom. 6:3-7). Thus, the number 8 seems to be symbolic of rebirth through baptism on earth (John 3:5; Moses 6:59).

The number 42 seems to be used in like manner. It conveys a message that all kindreds of the earth may be blessed with the blessings of the gospel, which are the blessings of salvation, even of eternal life, if they go out of spiritual Babylon, are baptized by water and by the Spirit, and receive the Melchizedek Priesthood, and that the gospel is the means of judging the nations in the *hour* of judgment (Abr. 2:11; D&C 84:33-34; 101:4-5; Rev. 14:6-7; 2 Ne. 25:22). As a means of helping mortal man to remember this message, there are 42 *generations* from Abraham until Christ, 42 *months* in Jesus' gospel ministry from baptism to crucifixion, and approximately 42 *years* in an *hour* of the Lord's time (2 Pet. 3:8). Thus, 42 relates to the *power* of eternal life derived from the *Melchizedek Priesthood* (3 x 14).

Days
A day conveys the idea of *faithfulness* or *obedience* to the word of God. This is seen as follows:

> "The Gods...organized and formed the heavens and the earth.... And they watched those things which they had ordered until they obeyed" (Abr. 4:1, 18).

A day is one rotation of the earth on its axis. The axis is an imaginary line like an iron rod, and an iron rod is like the word of God (1 Ne. 15:24). Since the earth rotates faithfully on its axis according to the word of God, it is obedient to the word of God (D&C 88:25).

Weeks
A week has its origin in the 6 days of creation and a

7th day wherein God finished his work and formed man out of the dust of the earth; and in the 7th thousand year period of the earth's temporal existence, God will complete his work pertaining to the salvation of man (D&C 77:6, 12). Thus, the number 7 seems to denote *fulness*.[2] This same meaning is also seen in John's description of the book which he saw, written within and on the back side, and sealed with 7 seals (Rev 5:1). It was *filled* with the revealed will, mysteries, and the works of God concerning this earth during the 7 thousand years of its *full* temporal existence (D&C 77:6-7). When the *6th seal* was opened, John saw 7 signs which caused fear to come upon all people denoted by 7 kinds of people (Rev. 6:12-17). The number 7 might therefore be used as a *fulness factor*.

Lucifer, a high ranking official, rebelled and thus fell short of a fulness. He became the father of lies, and sought to deceive and blind men, and to lead them captive at his will (Moses 4:3-4). The number 6 (just short of 7) has come to be associated with him and the great chain by which he veils the heavens with darkness (Moses 7:26). Darkness symbolizes Satan's temptations (1 Ne. 12:17). Darkness came at the 6th hour on crucifixion day, testifying that men had yielded to his temptations and crucified the Lord (Matt. 27:45).

If the numbers 1, 2, and 3 refer to the Father, the Son, and the Holy Ghost, then in the above context the number 6, as $1 \times 2 \times 3$, implies that Satan rebelled against the Father, wanted the position held by Jeho-

---

[2]J. R. Dummelow, *The One Volume Bible Commentary* [New York: MacMillan Publishing Co., Inc., 35th ed., 1973], pp. 1072-73.

vah, and sought to use the Spirit to compel others to do his will. Satan's power is limited. He has power over us only to the extent that we do not accept the invitation to pray unto the Father (1), in the name of Jesus Christ (2), by the power of the Spirit (3) (Eph. 2:18).

Two weeks (2 x 7 *days* = 14 *days*) of the Lord's time comprise the combined period of the earth's *physical creation* and *temporal existence* (D&C 77:6, 12). Without the Creation and the Fall, the blessing of eternal life would be impossible. We had to leave our premortal home to be added upon (Abr. 3:26), to be tried and tested, and to be married by an everlasting covenant (D&C 131:1-4). Honoring the everlasting marriage covenant enables us to be added upon forever and ever (Abr. 3:26; D&C 132:19). Jacob was taught this lesson by the same numerical means used to teach Abraham the doctrine of accountability. Jacob had to leave home and labor *14 years* to receive his wives, 7 years for Leah (*wearied*) and 7 years for Rachel (*ewe* or *sheep*) (Gen. 28:2-4; 29:20-28). Jacob's faithfulness has enabled his exaltation (D&C 132:37). (See also Paul's witness in Gal. 1:15-24; 2:1.) The number 14 (7 x 2) seems to reference the *fulness* of the Priesthood after the order of the *Son of God* (D&C 107:2-3).

The Fall brought death into the world (Gen. 2:16-17). Without the Atonement and Resurrection, mankind would have been lost forever (Alma 34:9-10; 11:40-44). The number 14 is 4 x 3.5. *Four* references the *whole earth*, and 4 x 3.5 references the *geographical completeness* of the *Atonement* brought about by Jesus Christ and the Priesthood authority which he held. The Atonement claims the penitent and brings to pass the

Resurrection, which brings men back into the presence of God to be judged (Alma 42:23). The number 3.5 is midway toward 7. Jesus Christ was *cut off* after a ministry of 3.5 years symbolic of his standing between us and a fulness of justice (Mosiah 15:8-9). Let us therefore use the number 3.5 as a *reconciliation factor*.[3]

Celestial marriage is an earthly ordinance which is performed by the Priesthood after the order of the Son of God (D&C 84:19-20). This suggests that 42, as 3 x 14, or perhaps better seen as 3 x 7 x 2, represents the eternal *power* of the *fulness* of the Holy Priesthood after the order of the *Son of God*. This Priesthood is called the Melchizedek Priesthood to avoid the frequent repetition of the name of God's Son (D&C 107:1-4). As 3 x 14, the number 42 also conveys a message that the *powers* of heaven are inseparably connected to the rights of the *Priesthood* (D&C 121:36), and that granting the gift of the *Holy Ghost* is a *Melchizedek Priesthood* function (D&C 20:68).

As noted at the beginning of this chapter, there were 14 generations from Abraham to David and 14 generations from David until the carrying away into Babylon, and 14 generations from the carrying away into Babylon until Christ (Matt. 1:17). When *genera-tions* are used as the unit of measure, 3 x 14 conveys a message that those who receive the Priesthood are to be clean; they are called to go out from Babylon, from the midst of wickedness, which is spiritual Babylon (D&C 133:5, 14). If they magnify their calling in the

---

[3]Richard D. Draper, *Opening the Seven Seals* [Salt Lake City: Deseret Book Company, 1991], p. 121.

Priesthood, they are sanctified by the *Spirit* unto the renewing of their bodies; they become the *seed of Abraham* and *kingdom of God* (D&C 84:33-34; Moses 6:60; D&C 20:79). The seed of Abraham is defined in Jehovah's blessing to Abraham:

> "My name is Jehovah, and I know the end from the beginning; therefore my hand shall be over thee. And I will make of thee a great nation, and I will bless thee above measure, and make thy name great among all nations, and thou shalt be a blessing unto thy seed after thee, that in their hands they shall bear this ministry and Priesthood unto all nations; And I will bless them through thy name; for as many as receive this Gospel shall be called after thy name, and shall be accounted thy seed, and shall rise up and bless thee, as their father; And I will bless them that bless thee, and curse them that curse thee; and in thee (that is, in thy Priesthood) and in thy seed (that is, thy Priesthood), for I give unto thee a promise that this right shall continue in thee, and in thy seed after thee (that is to say, the literal seed, or the seed of the body) shall all the families of the earth be blessed, even with the blessings of the Gospel, which are the blessings of salvation, even of life eternal." (Abr. 2:8-11.)

Months

Months are derived from the moon's orbital periods. The moon waxes and wanes from darkness into light and again into darkness. From Moses' time, Israel used a lunar calendar. The first day of a new moon was the first day of a new month so that a month consisted of either 29 or 30 days (BD p. 628).[4] The cycle of feasts began in the first ecclesiastical month called Abib (later Nisan). The 14th day of Abib was set to coincide with a full moon to remind Israel of the passover (Smith's Bible Dictionary, "Month"). In the symbolism of John's vision recorded in Revelation, a woman (the church) brought forth the political kingdom.   When the kingdom was caught up unto God, the woman, like the moon, went into the wilderness of darkness (Rev. 12:5, 10). In the day of restoration the church, again like the moon, comes out of darkness and brings forth the millennial kingdom (D&C 1:30; 65; 84:34; 109:73).

Years
The root meaning of the Hebrew word for *year* is *change.*[5] A year represents a *change of seasons* as the earth orbits the Sun and *returns.*[6] Therefore, it seems appropriate to view *years* as being symbolic of *return, redemption,* or *restoration.* Through the Atonement and Resurrection mankind may return and live in God's

---

[4]The center of mass of the earth-moon system is located about 1061 miles below the earth's surface. With respect to the Sun, the moon's orbit is one *synodic* month of 29.53 days (the month of phases). With respect to the stars, the moon orbits this barycenter in 27.32 days (a *sidereal* month). This is also the *synchronous* rotational period, hence, we see only one hemisphere of the moon—the face of the "man in the moon." This 27.32 days relates to the symbolic number 3^3 (see p. 83).

[5]Hastings Dictionary of the Bible, "Year".

[6]The four seasons arise because the earth's equatorial plane is inclined 23.5° to the ecliptic.

presence, if faithful. In the beginning of the 7000th *year* period, the Lord will a) sanctify the earth, b) complete the salvation of man, and c) judge all things. The number 7 in 7000 conveys the idea of a *fulness*. The number 10 denotes *temporal* or *finite* *completeness*,[7] or the *whole* of a part.[8] The number 1000 (10^3) conveys the idea of *divine completeness* or the *omnipotence* of the *Spirit*. The third power also alludes to the three concepts noted in a, b, and c above. *Years* imply that the Lord will *redeem* all things, except that which he has not put into his *power*. (D&C 77:12.)

The Length of Jesus' Life and Ministry
The "heaven" was shut in the days of Elijah and there was famine "throughout all the land" for 3.5 years (Luke 4:25). The Atonement enables the *windows of heaven* to be opened when sincere *offerings* are made unto the Father in the name of Jesus Christ (Mal. 3:10). The 3.5-year (42-month, 180-week, 1260-day) length of Jesus' ministry from baptism to crucifixion would be a reminder to Israel of this fact. *Years* remind us that the Bridegroom is the Redeemer; *months* (moon) reference the bride (the church) that brings forth the political kingdom; *weeks* reference a fulness; and *days* remind us that Jesus set the example of obedience by the things which he suffered (Heb. 5:8).

---

[7] Smith's Bible Dictionary, "Number"; cf. Moses 8:27.

[8] For example, the Ten Tribes or the Ten Commandments; Richard D. Draper, *Opening the Seven Seals* [Salt Lake City: Deseret Book Company, 1991], p. 123.

Jesus was baptized in his 30th year—when he began to be about 30 years old (Luke 3:23; cf. Nu. 4:3). It would have been in a "harvest" month, in the Fall of AD 29.

The 1260 days of Jesus' ministry fit Daniel's "time and times and the dividing of a time" according to John (Dan. 7:25; compare Rev. 12:6 and Rev. 12:14). Therefore, the three periods in Jesus' 1260-day ministry are 360 days corresponding to a "time", 720 days corresponding to "times", and 180 days corresponding to the "dividing of a time" or "half a time". If Jesus was born on Thursday, 6 April 1 BC, lived 12,048 days,[9] and died on Friday, AD 1 April 33,[10] the three periods of his ministry would have been as follows:

The 180-day period would have begun with Jesus' baptism (on Saturday, AD 20 October 29). John began baptizing in the 15th year of the reign of Tiberias (Luke 3:1) during the feast of Tabernacles, a harvest festival symbolic of the harvest of souls. This period included the temptations and the first cleansing of the temple, up until Wednesday, AD 17 April 30.

The 720-day period would have begun on Thursday, AD 18 April 30, and gone through Tuesday, AD 6 April 32.

---

[9]The Nephites counted 12,048 days from the time they saw the sign of Jesus' birth (3 Ne. 1:15-22) until the time they saw the sign of his death (3 Ne. 8:5). They were using 365 days per year.

[10]James E. Talmage, *Jesus the Christ* [Salt Lake City: Deseret Book Company, 41st Ed., 1974], p. 104; John P. Pratt, *Ensign*, Jun. 1985, pp. 67-8; Jan. 1994, pp. 42-3; CR 1973, Apr:4; 1975, Apr:3-4).

The 360-day period ("a time") in Christ's ministry would have begun on Wednesday, AD 7 April 32, and includes the second cleansing of the temple, and most importantly, the Atonement which ended with the crucifixion on Friday, AD 1 April 33. Three days later, counting *inclusively*, Jesus Christ was resurrected. This was Sunday, AD 3 April 33.

Jesus' death after a ministry of 3 x 14 *months* is a reminder that with Jesus' death on the *14th day* of Abib and his resurrection on the *third day* thereafter the law of Moses was fulfilled and the kingdom of God was born. The woman to whom John the Revelator referred, like the moon, waxed toward a fulness and brought it forth (JST Rev. 12:3-5); but the kingdom would be taken away and the enemy would plant tares among the wheat. As a result the woman would wane and go into the wilderness of darkness. But in the day of *restoration* she would come out of the wilderness of darkness and wax toward a fulness and again bring forth the kingdom through a messenger identified by 3 x 14 30-*year* periods (D&C 1:29-30).

Jesus' death after a ministry of 6 x 7 *months* implies that on the 6th *day* as the 7th *day* approached, darkness came and the moon (woman) literally appeared as blood (Acts 2:20),[11] symbolic of the

---

[11]Eclipses in the earth-moon system depend upon the orientation of the lines of nodes of the moon's inclined orbit (5.15° to the ecliptic), since the moon must be near the ecliptic plane (a) to pass directly between the Sun and the earth in a solar eclipse, and (b) to pass through the earth's shadow in a lunar eclipse. The lines of nodes must point toward the Sun if an eclipse is to occur.

kingdom's birth. Darkness came at noon, the 6th hour, symbolic of the darkness caused by Satan's great chain (Moses 7:56, 26). It last until the 9th hour (Matt. 27:45). The 3^2 hour (9th hour) emphasizes two messages heard in two *loud* cries of the Savior: "My God, my God, why has thou forsaken me" (Matt. 27:46)? The *Spirit* withdrew to enable Jesus to complete the Atonement by himself so that all mankind *could be* saved by him on conditions of repentance (D&C 18:11-12; Alma 11:40-41). Jesus cried again and yielded up the *ghost* to enable him to bring about the Resurrection so that all mankind *would be* resurrected, unconditionally (Matt. 27:50-53; Alma 11:42-44).

In *months* 9 references physical birth, the spirit joining with the body; the 9th *hour* references the hour of death, when spirit and body separate, and the light of life begins to shine in the spirit world (D&C 138:18). The sum 8R + 1R = 9R, where R is the radius of a circle, references rebirth through baptism into the kingdom of God on earth (8R) (Moses 6:59) and return to God in heaven (1R) (D&C 76:62). Since 8 equals 1 x 2 x 4 a message is also given that the kingdom of God and his Christ shall fill the whole earth (Dan. 2:35), for the earth shall be celestialized (D&C 88:25-26).

John's 1260 Years Point to Joseph Smith
After the Atonement and Resurrection, the *woman* brought forth the kingdom of God and his Christ (Rev. 12:10); but it was taken from the earth, and the woman fled into the wilderness. To show *who* would lead the woman (church) out of the wilderness of darkness and obscurity (D&C 1:30), John referred to 1260 years:

"And the woman...brought forth a man child,...and her child was caught up unto God and his throne.... And the woman fled into the wilderness, where she had a place prepared of God, that they should feed her there a thousand two hundred and threescore years" (JST Rev. 12:3-5).

The King James Version says *days* (Rev. 12:6), but Joseph Smith replaced *days* with *years* (JST Rev. 12:5). It appears that 1260 *years* is to be used in a *restoration* and *return* context for those who have ears to understand by the Spirit (Rev. 2:7, 17; Rom. 10:17).

The 1260-Year Cornerstone

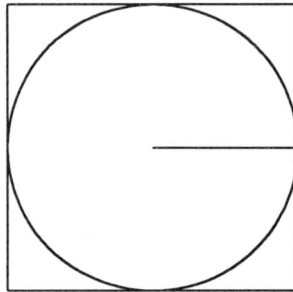

Diagram 1.1

A squared circle is symbolic of man's progression from the midst of eternity (center of circle) to earth (square), through earth life, and return to God. The product 9R in the squared circle references physical birth made possible by the Fall, and spiritual birth and return to God made possible by the Atonement and Resurrection. If the circumference of the circle in Diagram 1.1 is 1260 years, Joseph Smith's birth year is revealed. The radius (R) of the 1260-year circle is 200.54 years, thus 9R equals 1804.86 years. If we use 6 April 1 BC as the reference point, this is AD 1805, Joseph Smith's birth year. The numerical value of the English form of the Hebrew tetragram YHWH in this 1260-year cornerstone is also 1805 years (p. 49). This equality also suggests that Joseph Smith and the everlasting covenant he promulgated is Jehovah's latter-day messenger (Mal. 3:1; D&C 45:9). When 9R is written as 1R years + 8R years, or better seen as 1^3R_{1260} *years* + 2^3R_{1260} *years*, the message relates to the witness, through the power of the Spirit, that Joseph Smith would receive of the Father and of the Son, and that through him the gospel taught during Jesus' 1260-*day* ministry would be restored (2 Ne. 3:11).

The radius (R) pointing to the 9th hour (3:00 p.m.) references both the Atonement of Jesus Christ and the Spirit (pp. 13, 19-20). The gift of the Holy Ghost is received through confirmation after baptism. The Holy Ghost brings the teachings of Jesus Christ to remembrance and guides worthy saints on earth (the square) into all truth or words of God necessary to obtain eternal life in eternity (the circle) (John 14:26; 16:13; 17:3; D&C 84:43-48).

Jesus Christ is the Chief Cornerstone (Ps. 118:21-22; Is. 28:16; Zech. 10:4; Eph. 2:20). He is the *sure foundation* (Hel. 5:12) upon which the builders of the latter-day kingdom have built. There is no other name given nor any other way nor means whereby salvation can come. Through spiritual birth into his kingdom, we become his sons and daughters (Mosiah 3:17; 5:7-8; Moses 6:59).

The 1260 years (3 x 14 30-*year* periods) prophesied by John (JST Rev. 12:5) convey a message regarding the *return* of the kingdom. The heavens would open again, and after being quickened by the *Spirit*, a 14-year old boy would see the Father and the Son. Three x 14 *months* after seeing Deity an angel would appear to the boy and reveal a record containing the fulness of the gospel of Jesus Christ to enable the woman to come out of the wilderness (D&C 1:29-30). As to the time of year this "harvesting" angel would come, it would be 180 days or *half a time* different from the time of year that the heavens were opened. Two *Priesthoods* would then be restored 14 *days* apart to enable the *faithful* to be sanctified by the *Spirit* unto the renewing of their bodies (D&C 84:33). Those who would receive these two Priesthoods, and magnify their calling, would become the seed of Abraham and kingdom of God (D&C 84:34; Abr. 2:11).

The 42 or 6 x 7 30-*year* periods implies that this *restoration* would come toward the end of the Lord's 6th *day* as the 7th *day* approached. In that day Satan would rage in the hearts of men (2 Ne. 28:20). Before the day of the Lord would come, the Sun would be darkened and the moon (woman) turned to blood (Rev. 6:12), symbolic of the birth of the millennial kingdom.

A Marvelous Symbolic Rallying Message

John's reference to 1260 *years* sends a marvelous symbolic rallying message to dispersed and scattered Israel that Joseph Smith is the modern link to the 1260-*day* ministry of Jesus Christ as recorded in the stick of Judah and in the stick of Ephraim (Ez. 37:16).

The dates of key restoration events were set forever in the Chief Cornerstone referred to by the prophets (i.e., Eph. 2:20). Matthew's record of Jesus' Abrahamic descent, and John's reference to the woman in the wilderness 1260 *years* and his correlation of 1260 to Jesus' ministry and to Daniel's "time and times and the dividing of a time" lead directly to this conclusion.

The Beginning and Ending of Christ's Mortal Ministry
Jesus' gospel ministry began with his baptism and the testimony of the Godhead (Matt. 3:13-17). It ended with his crucifixion and the testimony of his creations and even of Satan: While Jesus was on the cross, there was darkness for 3 *hours* (Matt. 27:45), testifying that the Son of God was being put to death by evil men who were walking in darkness at noon-day (i.e., Matt. 26:21-26; Luke 22:1-6; D&C 95:6). As he died, the earth also spoke for 3 *hours* in the form of storms, tempests, thunderings, lightnings, and earthquakes (Matt. 27:51; 3 Ne. 8:5-19), testifying that the God of nature suffers (1 Ne. 19:12). And finally, Satan spoke for 3 *days* in the form of "mists of darkness", testifying that his great chain held evil men captive—they had yielded to his temptations and crucified the Lord (1 Ne. 12:17).

Jesus' genealogical record testifies that he is the *Way* out of spiritual Babylon and into the fold of God where the blessings of Abraham are available through an enduring faithfulness (Abr. 2:11; D&C 84:33-38; 101:4-5; 132:19). It *invokes* the entire gospel plan similar to a gospel *merism* (Noel Reynolds, *BYU Studies*, 31/3/91, pp. 31-50). It taps into the well of living waters which never cease (John 4:14; Moses 1:4).

Chapter 2

GOSPEL SYMBOLISM

> Symbols are the universal language in which all gospel ordinances and covenants are revealed. "God teaches with symbols; it is his favorite way of teaching" (Orson F. Whitney, *Improvement Era*, August 1927, 851).

Jesus Christ came from the "bosom of eternity" (D&C 88:13) to show us the way; and he declared: "No man cometh unto the Father, but by me" (John 14:6). "I am the light of the world: he that followeth me shall not walk in darkness" (John 8:12). "God doth not walk in crooked paths, neither doth he turn to the right hand nor to the left, neither doth he vary from that which he hath said, therefore his paths are *straight*, and his course is *one eternal round*" (D&C 3:2; italics added). The word of God is truth (D&C 84:45); it is like an iron rod to which one must cling to pass through successfully the mists of darkness symbolic of Satan's temptations (1 Ne. 12:17; 15:24). From a diagrammatical viewpoint, truth or the word of God is represented by a straight line (—), and eternity by a circle (O).

In referring to the latter-day gathering of Israel and Judah, Isaiah said: "And he shall set up an ensign for the nations, and shall assemble the outcasts of Israel, and gather together the dispersed of Judah from the *four corners of the earth*" (Is. 11:12; italics added). John the Revelator saw four angels standing on the *four corners of the earth* (Rev. 7:1). The earth is therefore represented diagrammatically by a square (□); and a mountain, where the word of God (truth) is revealed from God to man on earth (i.e., 1 Ne. 11:1), is represented by a square-based pyramid (△).

The Earth in Eternity

"Whereupon are the foundations thereof fastened? or who laid the corner stone thereof" (Job 38:5-7)? The earth is "fastened" to eternity (our galaxy), represented by the square and the circle, respectively. Jehovah is Father of heaven and earth (Mosiah 3:8), the Light which governs and gives life (D&C 88:6-13; JST John 1:4-5). He is the Resurrection and the Life (John 11:25), and the Chief Cornerstone of the Church (Eph. 2:20), represented by a squared circle, which is also symbolic of man's progression from the midst of eternity to earth, into the Church, and on to eternity.

> "And I, the Lord God, planted a garden eastward in Eden, and there I put the man whom I had formed. And out of the ground made I, the Lord God, to grow every tree... And I, the Lord God, planted the tree of life also in the midst of the garden, and also the tree of knowledge of good and evil. And I, the Lord God, caused a *river* to go out of Eden to water the garden; and from thence it was parted, and became into four heads [four branches]" (Moses 3:8-10; footnote 10b, Gen. 2; italics added).

Think of a river as coming down from above the page to the center point of Diagram 2.1 and dividing into four branches forming a cruciform. The river carries living water (John 4:10, 14; 7:38-39; 1 Ne. 11:25), symbolic of God's words which never cease (Moses 1:4; 6:62). The word of God is the gospel which is with the Son (JST John 1:1). Let the lines of the cruciform represent the first principles and ordinances of his gospel—faith in Jesus Christ, repentance, baptism, and the gift of the Holy Ghost (A of F 1:4). After Adam and Eve partook of the forbidden fruit, God "placed at the east of the Garden of Eden, cherubim and a flaming sword, which turned every way to keep the way of the tree of life" (Moses 4:31). The flaming sword is symbolic of the justice of God (1 Ne. 15:30). The partaking of the forbidden fruit brought death into the world, both spiritual and temporal (Moses 3:16-17; Alma 12:12-37). Adam and Eve were then taught the gospel and plan of salvation (Moses 6:48-63) that they might learn obedience in the face of opposition and eventually be enabled to "pass by the angels...which are set there, to their exaltation and glory in all things... which glory shall be a fulness and a continuation of the seeds forever and ever" (D&C 132:19).

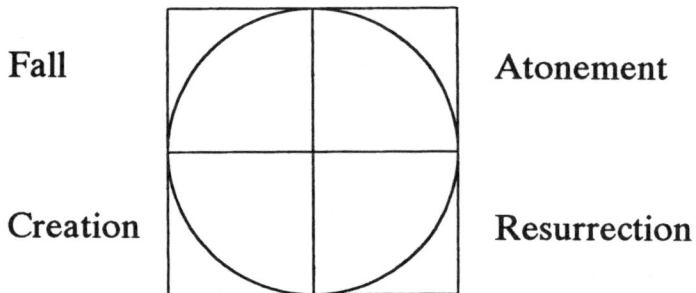

Fall   Atonement

Creation   Resurrection

Diagram 2.1

Beginning in the bottom left-hand quadrant and going clockwise in Diagram 2.1, let the quadrants represent the Creation, the Fall, the Atonement, and the Resurrection, respectively. The Atonement of Jesus Christ appeases the demands of justice (Alma 42:15) and on conditions of repentance mankind may overcome spiritual death and obtain eternal life in eternity represented by the inscribed circle (Alma 11:40-41; D&C 18:10-12). Temporal death is overcome, unconditionally, by virtue of the Atonement and Resurrection of Jesus Christ (Alma 11:42-44).

The Year of the First Vision
The cornerstone shown in Diagram 2.1 gives the year of the First Vision when an event which occurred at the crucifixion is used in combination with the abomination of desolation prophecy (BD, p. 601). Matthew wrote:

> "Now from the sixth hour [noon] there was *darkness over all the land* unto the ninth hour [3:00 p.m.]" (Matt. 27:45; italics added).

To visualize how this event relates to the First Vision, let us draw a circle in the Atonement quadrant of Diagram 2.1 and assign to it a circumference equal to the *temporal existence* of the earth, namely, 7000 years (D&C 77:6) (see Diagram 2.2). The circle would then represent temporal time. The exact cause of the darkness which overshadowed the land at noonday is not clear. It appears that there was a lunar eclipse on crucifixion day which caused the moon to appear as blood and to go into the wilderness of darkness.[1]

The darkness "over all the land" from the 6th to the 9th hours is symbolic of the *spiritual darkness* that would be "over all the land" from the time of the abomination of desolation to the First Vision. Shortly before the crucifixion, the Lord said to the Apostles,

---

[1]John P. Pratt, *Ensign*, June 1985, pp. 64-65.

"When you, therefore, shall see the abomination of desolation spoken of by Daniel the prophet, concerning the destruction of Jerusalem, then you shall stand in the holy place; whoso readeth let him understand. Then let them who are in Judea flee into the mountains" (JS-M 1:12-13). In AD 70—seventy years after the face of the Son of Man was first seen by Joseph, Mary's espoused husband—a Roman army under Titus completely destroyed Jerusalem and the temple in accordance with Daniel's prophecy.

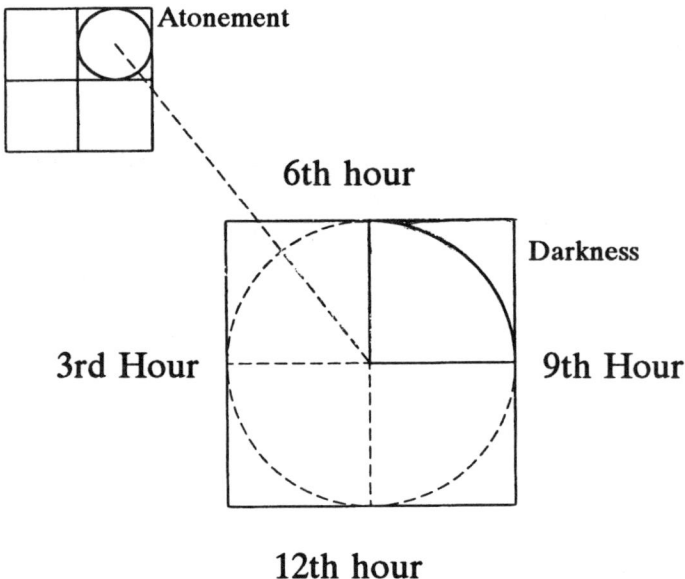

Atonement

6th hour

Darkness

3rd Hour

9th Hour

12th hour

0, 7000 years

Diagram 2.2

The length of the arc from the 6th to the 9th hour is 1750 years. If 1750 years is added to AD 70, the year of the abomination of desolation, the result is AD 1820, the year when a latter-day Joseph among the Gentiles first saw the *face* of the Son of Man. Seventy *years* later (AD 1890) the Son of Man *turned back* his *face* toward Israel (Lev. 26:17; Hosea 6:2; D&C 130:15; *History of the Church*, 5:336, hereafter cited as "HC"). Before AD 1890, the Lord "sent [his] everlasting covenant into the world, to be a light to the world, and to be a standard for [his] people, and for the Gentiles [who sit in darkness] to seek to it, and to be a messen- ger before [his] *face* to prepare the way before [him]" (D&C 45:9).

The Meridian of Time
Enoch asked the Lord, "When shall the day of the Lord come? When shall the blood of the righteous be shed...? And the Lord said: It shall be in the *meridian of time*" (Moses 7:45-46). Meridian is "midday" or "high point." Therefore, the meridian of time would be: sunrise (the middle of the day of darkness and light), noon (the middle of the day of light) (Gen. 1:1-5),[2] and Son rise (the beginning of a new day in the Lord's week). Jesus is the *Light of the world* (John 8:12). He would be born at sunrise, at the beginning of a new millennium (D&C 77:6), and be crucified at noon as darkness covered the land (Matt. 27:45; D&C 95:6). The Light would rise again the first day of the week (Matt. 28:1-6; cf. Gen. 1:3; 3 Ne. 10:9).

---

[2]John P. Pratt, *Ensign*, January 1994, p. 39.

The Chief Cornerstone of the Restored Kingdom

"The stone which the builders refused has become the headstone of the corner" (JST Ps. 118:22; cf. Zech. 10:4). Jesus Christ is the Chief Cornerstone of the kingdom (Is. 28:16; Eph. 2:20). President Gordon B. Hinckley outlined four cornerstones of the *restored* kingdom, sub-cornerstones which fit within the Chief Cornerstone, namely, Joseph Smith, the First Vision, the Book of Mormon, and Apostles and Prophets.[3]

From Diagrams 2.1 and 2.2, let us draw a 1260-unit circle, symbolic of Jesus' 1260-day ministry, and inscribe it in a square with a cruciform. This provides a chief cornerstone for the restored kingdom of God in the dispensation of the fulness of times (Diagram 2.3).

A Chief Cornerstone
of the Restored Kingdom of God

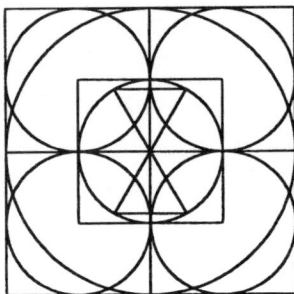

0, 1260 units

Diagram 2.3

[3]Gordon B. Hinckley, *Faith, the Essence of True Religion* [Salt Lake City: Deseret Book Company, 1989], pp. 7-12; see Chapter 13.

Joseph Smith's birth year is given by 9R in the 1260-*year* cornerstone (pp. 14-15). The length in months of a woman's expectancy before giving physical birth was apparently set by the Creator to correlate with 9R in the squared circle so that the teachings of the Fall and physical birth and death, and of the Atonement and spiritual birth and death would be set forever in geometrical symbolism (Moses 6:59; D&C 29:40-45).

Let the 4 lines forming the cruciform in Diagram 2.3 represent the first principles and ordinances of the gospel, namely, faith in the Lord Jesus Christ, repentance, baptism by immersion for the remission of sins, and laying on of hands for the gift of the Holy Ghost; and let the 4 lines which form the outer square (8R), represent 8 *elements* of the baptismal covenant (Mosiah 18:8-10). Four sub-cornerstones fit within the 1260-unit cornerstone. They have 630-unit inscribed circles. Their centers are tied together by 4 lines forming an inner square. The lines forming concentric squares imply a separation of the profane from the holy. Moving inward gives a sense of removing oneself from the world, but still being in the world. Moving upward, as square planes in a pyramid, gives a sense of separation of things which are below from things which are above. Let the 4 lines forming the inner square represent the "laws," "covenants," or "words of eternal life" (D&C 84:43-48). The inner square has a 630-unit inscribed circle and two equilateral triangles, one in the lower semicircle pointing upward ($\triangle$) and one in the upper semicircle pointing downward ($\triangledown$). They are placed on top of one another so that their points touch at the center point of the circle. They represent the *physical* and *spiritual* planes, and in this position are sometimes abbreviated simply by an X. Combined or interlaced they form the six-pointed Creator's star (✡).

YHWH (Jehovah) and Alpha (∧) and Omega (Ω) signs are seen in the center square of Diagram 2.3. YHWH equals 1805 units, and YHWH + Alpha and Omega equal 2520 units (p. 49). In the four quadrants of Diagram 2.3 the phases of the moon are also seen, the waxing and waning crescents and the waxing and waning gibbous. This symbolizes the church coming out of the wilderness of darkness to shine forth fair as the moon and clear as the sun and terrible as an army with banners (or ensign) (D&C 109:73). The dates of key events pertaining to the restoration of the latter-day kingdom appear to have been set in this cornerstone.

Daniel, Nephi, and John the Revelator
Daniel (*judgment of God*) saw the coming of Christ, the crucifixion, the abomination of desolation, and the apostasy. He saw that Satan would have dominion through the kingdoms of the world and wear out the former-day saints, and their posterity would be "given into his hand until a time and times and the dividing of a time" (Dan. 7:25). He also saw the restoration of the kingdom of God in the latter-days (Dan. 2:44).

Nephi also saw in vision the restoration in the latter-days; and he learned that one of Jesus' Apostles whose name would be John (*Jehovah's gift*) would be charged to write about this kingdom in a manner which would be plain and easy to understand (1 Ne. 14:18-27).

In fulfillment of this prophecy, John, the Beloved Apostle, received a revelation of Jesus Christ which was signified[4] by an angel, and he was commanded to write the things which he saw (Rev. 1:1, 19). John wrote that he saw seven candlesticks representing seven churches in the Roman province of Asia (Rev. 1:20). The light coming from the seven candlesticks comes from burning pure olive oil placed in cup-shaped containers resting on top of each candlestick. The light is therefore representative of the Holy Spirit. In the midst of the seven candlesticks was "one like unto the Son of Man" out of whose mouth went "a sharp two-edged sword" (Rev. 1:13). The word of God is quick and powerful, sharper than a two-edged sword (D&C 6:2). It is truth (D&C 84:45). The wicked take the truth to be hard, for it cuts them to the very center (1 Ne. 16:2). The justice of God is as a flaming sword (1 Ne. 15:24, 30).

The Tree of Life Symbol
The seven candlestick symbol is also a tree of life symbol. It is a Jewish *menorah*.[5] The left-hand side of Diagram 2.4 shows a two-dimensional tree of life symbol in which is seen a seven candlestick symbol.

---

[4]A symbol is a *signifier* of something else by reason of a relationship or association with it (*Merriam-Webster's Collegiate Dictionary* [Springfield, Massachusetts, 10th ed.]). The meaning of a symbol is that which is *signified*. Jesus taught the multitudes in parables; and then to his disciples Jesus said: "It is given unto you to know the mysteries of the kingdom of heaven, but to them it is not given" (Matt. 13:11).

[5]Irwin Goodenough, *Jewish Symbols* [New York: Pantheon Books, 1953], Vol. 4, pp. 72-78.

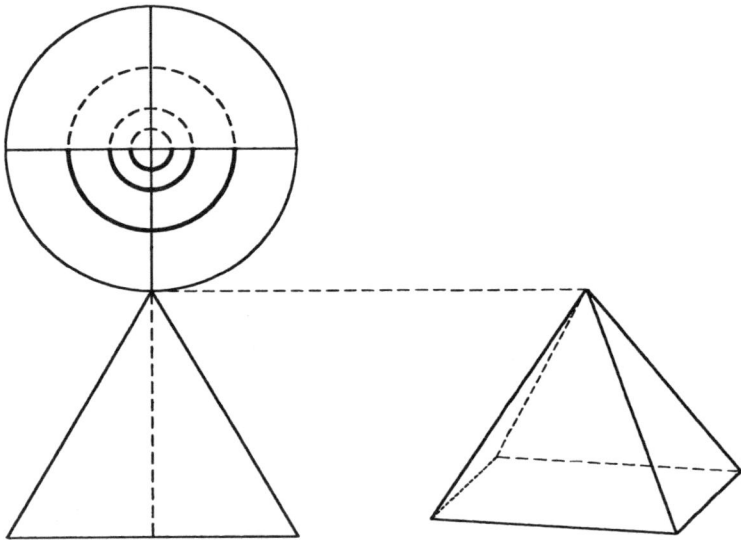

0, 1260 units

Diagram 2.4

The tree of life represents the love of God, or Jesus Christ, his Beloved Son (1 Ne. 11:9-25; cf. John 3:16). This symbol is defined by a "time and times and the dividing of a time", the sum of which fits Jesus' 1260-day ministry from baptism to crucifixion. The 1, ½, and ¼ relationship of the 720, 360, 180 addends of 1260 days conveys a message that through obedience to the gospel we may become one with the Father (1). Through the At-one-ment the Son submitted himself to the will of the Father (½), and when the trump sounds in the hour of judgment (D&C 88:103-104), all the world will bow the knee to the Father (¼) and confess that Jesus is the Christ. The outer circle of Diagram 2.4 is the 1260 circle; the next circles inward are the 720, 360, and 180 circles, respectively. These are wheels-within-wheels (Ez. 1:16). Table 1 shows their extension by the *fulness* and *reconciliation factors*.

Table 1

Time and Times and Dividing of a Time

360	x 7	=	2520	÷ 2	=	1260
720	x 7	=	5040	÷ 2	=	2520
180	x 7	=	1260	÷ 2	=	630
1260	x 7	=	8820	÷ 2	=	4410

The Son of Man stands in the midst of seven candlesticks; and out of his mouth comes a sharp two-edged sword (Rev. 1:13), symbolic of the word of God (Eph. 6:17; D&C 27:18). The word of God is carried by a *river*—a line extending vertically downward from the center of the concentric spheres to the center of the square base shown on the right side in Diagram 2.4. In three dimensions the equilateral triangle is a face of a square pyramid and the circles are spheres. The dashed vertical line is the length of a face of the pyramid, or, in two dimensions, the height of the triangle. The pyramid represents a *mountain* where light and truth are revealed from God to man (i.e., 1 Ne. 11:1). Light is the scepter of power (D&C 88:13; Num. 24:17), and truth is knowledge of things as they are, were, and will be (D&C 93:24). The keys of the kingdom are given unto man on earth, and from thence the gospel rolls forth as the *stone* which is cut out of the mountain (Dan. 2:34, 44-45; D&C 65:2)—the square base of the pyramid in Diagram 2.4 represents the Chief Corner*stone* from Diagram 2.3. The tree of life symbol also shows a number of Alpha ($\wedge$) and Omega (Ω) signs as the flaming sword turns every way.

The Numerical Constants Pi (π) and Phi (ϕ)
The faces of Egypt's Great Pyramid are nearly (not quite) equilateral triangles. Their dimensions were apparently set to reveal the phi constant ($\phi = 1.618$) in the ratio of the length of a face to one-half the length of the base. Phi has properties which allow for easy two-dimensional mapping of the earth's surface using phi's unique properties (i.e., $1 + \phi = \phi^2$; $1 + 1/\phi = \phi$; and $6/5 \times \phi^2 = \pi = 3.1416$).[6] Both π and ϕ are in the symbolism of the Chief Cornerstone as will be seen.

A Counting Procedure for Key Events
A procedure for *seeing* the dates of key events in the restoration of the Church is to follow the order of the sub-cornerstones in the Chief Cornerstone on a "line upon line and precept upon precept" basis (2 Ne. 28:30)—from Joseph Smith to the First Vision to the Book of Mormon to the Apostles and Prophets and so on (p. 24), using Jesus' birthday as the reference point. Days are counted *inclusively* (i.e., there are 3 days from the crucifixion on Friday to the resurrection on Sunday; the boundary days, Friday and Sunday, are counted).

---

[6]Peter Tompkins, *Secrets of the Great Pyramid* (New York: Harper & Row, Publishers, 1971), pp. 189-200.

Chapter 3

BIRTH OF JESUS CHRIST

> "Behold, a virgin shall be with child, and shall bring forth a son, and they shall call his name Emmanuel (which, being interpreted, is, God with us)" (JST Matt. 2:6; cf. Matt. 1:23).

Jesus referred to his body as a temple, but because of spiritual blindness the people thought he was referring to the Zerubbabel Temple[1] which had been rebuilt by Herod. This event occurred at passover subsequent to Jesus' first cleansing of the temple. With a scourge of small cords, Jesus had driven out the animals and money changers and overthrown the tables and said, "Take these things hence; make not my Father's house an house of merchandise" (John 2:16). In response the Jews asked: "What sign shewest thou unto us, seeing that thou doest these things" (John 2:18)? Jesus said:

> "Destroy this temple, and in three days I will raise it up. Then said the Jews, Forty and six years was this temple in building, and wilt thou rear it up in three days? But he spake of the temple of his body" (John 2:19-21; cf. 1 Cor. 6:19).

The temple of Jesus' body was destroyed on the last *day* of the 360-day period of his ministry, and he rose the third day, counting *inclusively*. Solomon's Temple was destroyed in 586 BC and 70 years later

---

[1]Zerubbabel means *born at Babel*. Zerubbabel was the head of the tribe of Judah at the time of the return from the Babylonian captivity in the first year of Cyrus. Upon the decree of Cyrus, Zerubbabel immediately set out to accomplish the task of rebuilding the temple in Jerusalem (BD p. 792).

(516 BC) the Zerubbabel Temple was dedicated (BD, p. 783). It was the first temple dedicated subsequent to the Babylonian captivity to which Matthew's genealogical record of the Savior refers. Just as Joseph Smith's birth year is set in the 1260-*year* cornerstone (pp. 13-15), Jesus' birth year is set in the 360-*year* cornerstone when using the dedication year of the Zerubbabel Temple as the reference point.

When the angel announced Jesus' birth to Mary, she wondered how she might endure the presence of God. The angel answered that the Spirit would make it possible (JST Luke 1:34-35). To calm Joseph's mind, the angel told Joseph not to worry about taking Mary to wife, for the child she carried was not of man; he was Jesus, the Savior of the world (JST Matt. 2:3-4).

The product $9R_{360}$ years gives the number of *years* from the dedication of the Zerubbabel Temple to the birth of Jesus Christ (Diagram 3.1). R_{360} years equals 57.3 years (360 years/2π); therefore, $9R_{360}$ years is 515 *years*. This gives Jesus' birth year as 1 BC. Since this result gives the number of years from the dedication of the Zerubbabel Temple to Jesus' birth, and since the antitype shows the same number of years from Jesus' birth to the destruction of the Temple in AD 70 as from the destruction of Solomon's Temple in 586 BC to the 516 BC dedication of the Zerubbabel Temple, a message is conveyed that Jesus was born to die for us. With R pointing to 3:00 p.m., the message references the Atonement of Christ and the eternal life in eternity (the circle) which is given to those who have faith in him, repent, are baptized and remain faithful to the end—the gospel *merism* (3 Ne. 27:16, 19-22).

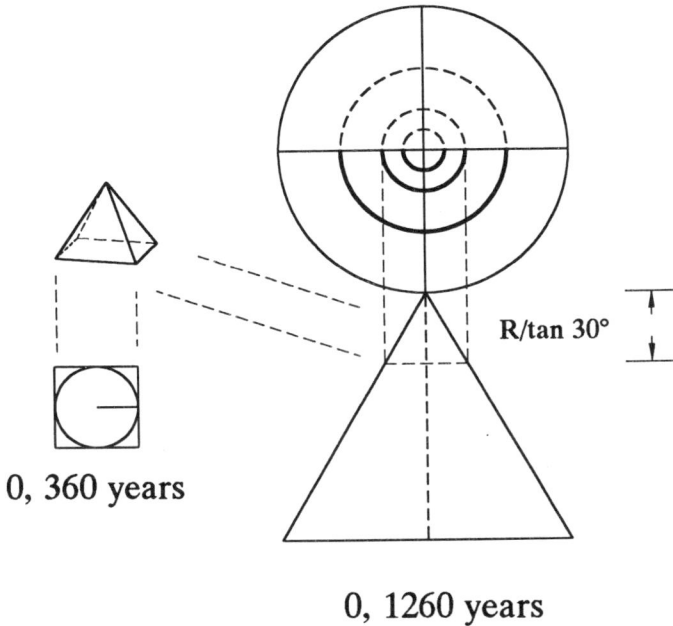

0, 360 years

R/tan 30°

0, 1260 years

Diagram 3.1

Eternal life is a gift to those who are obedient to the gospel and its associated covenants. Straight lines represent truth or the words of eternal life (D&C 84:43-48). The everlasting covenants are received on earth, a square represented by 8R. The sealing of covenants by the Holy Spirit of Promise is represented by 1R along the gift of the Holy Ghost line of the cruciform. The relationship 9R = 8R + 1R conveys a message that all who are *born* on earth and *reborn* into God's kingdom and receive the *gift of the Holy Ghost* "shall have hope through the atonement of Christ and the power of his resurrection, to be raised unto life eternal, and this because of [their] faith in him accord-

ing to the promise" (Moro. 7:41). This statement by
Mormon invokes the gospel *merism* (Noel Reynolds,
BYU Studies, 31/3/91, pp. 31-50).

Jesus' Birth Year From the Tree of Life Symbol
Jesus Christ is the Light of the world—he holds the
scepter of power (Num. 24:17; D&C 88:13). He is the
Stem of Jesse and Root of David (Is. 11:1; D&C 113:1-
2; Rev. 22:16). He was born King of the Jews (JST
Matt. 1:2-5). He came in a fulness of time (Gal. 4:4)
to restore the kingdom. A *restoration* in a fulness of
time is represented numerically by $7 \times 360\,years = 2520$
years. Using two dimensions, if the tree of life symbol
shown in Diagram 3.1 is expanded twofold so that the
circumference of the outer circle equals a fulness of
time (2520 years), and the beginning of Israel's regal
kingdom is used as the reference point, we have Jesus'
birth year. King Saul began his reign in 1095 BC,
probably near 1096 BC (BD p. 636). If we subtract
from 1096 BC the sum of the scepter line and the
height of the triangle, we have 1 BC.[2] Since Jesus
Christ is also Alpha and Omega, the same result may
be obtained from an Alpha and Omega sign (p. 51).

Jesus Descended Below All Things
The radius (R) in the tree of life symbol (Diagram 3.1)
equals ½ the base (B) of the triangle, suggesting that
the Son descended below all things in submitting

---

[2][1096 BC - (R_{2520} years + R_{2520} years/tan 30°) = 1 BC]. In
three dimensions, we would use the radius of a sphere and the length
of a face of a pyramid to obtain this result.

himself to the will of the Father (Moses 4:2). Of symbolic significance is the fact that Jesus was baptized in the Jordan River at a point about 1260 feet below sea level. Daniel's three term series of a time and times and the dividing of a time (Dan. 7:25) implies that in his submission the Savior would *knock* three times (in the garden of Gethsemane—Matt. 26:39, 42, 44), for the three term series has a 1, ½, and ¼ relationship. It conveys a message that the Son submitted himself to the will of the Father (½) and eventually all the world would bow the knee to the Father (¼) while they hear the sound of the trump, saying: "Fear God, and give glory to him who sitteth upon the throne, forever and ever; for the hour of his judgment is come" (D&C 88:104). Daniel means *judgment of God*, and the gospel taught during Jesus' 1260-day ministry is the means of judging the nations in the hour of judgment (2 Ne. 25:22). In the tree of life symbol (Diagram 2.4), Daniel's three term series is seen in the 720, 360, and 180 circles. In the cornerstone shown in Diagram 2.3, it is seen in the 1260, 630, and 315 circles.

The Birthday of Jesus the Christ

When in 1 BC was Jesus born? The Lord said: "It shall be in the meridian of time..." (Moses 7:45-46). In 1 BC the meridian day of the meridian month of the Hebrew secular year was 6 April. It is thus assumed that Jesus Christ was born on Thursday, 6 April 1 BC.[3]

---

[3]James E. Talmage, *Jesus the Christ* [Salt Lake City: Deseret Book Company, 41st ed., 1974], p. 104; *Ensign*, May 1980, p. 54; June 1985, pp. 67-68; Jan. 1994, pp. 42-43; May 1997, p. 53.

Chapter 4

BIRTH OF JOSEPH SMITH

> "Joseph truly testified, saying: A seer shall the Lord raise up... And his name shall be called after me;... And he shall be like unto me; for the thing, which the Lord shall bring forth by his hand...shall bring my people unto salvation" (2 Ne. 3:6, 15).

Joseph of old was sold into Egypt by his brothers (Gen. 37:26-28). While he was there, Pharaoh had a dream which Joseph interpreted as follows:

> "Behold, there come seven years of great plenty throughout all the land of Egypt: And there shall arise after them seven years of famine; and all the plenty shall be forgotten in the land of Egypt; and the famine shall consume the land; And the plenty shall not be known in the land by reason of that famine following; for it shall be very grievous" (Gen. 41:29-31).

Joseph warned Pharaoh "to look out a man discreet and wise, and set him over the land of Egypt. Let Pharaoh do this, and let him appoint officers over the land, and take up the fifth part of the land of Egypt in the seven plenteous years. And let them gather all the food of those good years that come, and lay up corn under the hand of Pharaoh, and let them keep food in the cities. And that food shall be for a store to the land against the seven years of famine." (Gen. 41:33-36.) Pharaoh followed Joseph's admonition and there was food in Egypt during the seven years of famine.

When Jacob heard there was food in Egypt, he sent his sons to buy grain. There they met Joseph. Eventually, Pharaoh invited Jacob and his family to dwell in Egypt and to eat of the fat of the land. Counting himself there were 66 members of Jacob's household who went into Egypt. Joseph was already there with his wife and two sons, making 4. Therefore, the total that the Lord brought into Egypt of Jacob's household was 70 (Gen. 46:26-27).

Subsequent to the Egyptian captivity, the house of Israel returned to their own land and became a great kingdom. But through disobedience the kingdom was divided into the Northern Kingdom headed by Ephraim and the Southern Kingdom headed by Judah. These kingdoms were destroyed by the Assyrians and Babylonians, respectively. The Ten Tribes were lost and the remainder of Ephraim was dispersed among the nations of the Gentiles through intermarriage as foreseen in prophecy (Gen. 48:19; 49:1; Hosea 7:8). The Jewish remnant was scattered and dispersed among all nations. Today, the natural branches of the house of Israel consist of the Jews, the Lamanites, and the Lost Tribes.

Many Gentiles came to America where the gospel was restored among them (1 Ne. 13:12-14, 39-40). In 1823 Moroni told Joseph Smith that the *fulness of the Gentiles* was about to come into the gospel covenant (JS-H 1:41). The *fulness of the Gentiles* refers to the literal seed of Israel and of Abraham *within* the Gentile people brought about through intermarriage, and to the seed of Israel or of Abraham (the Priesthood) *among* the Gentile people (Abr. 2:11). The number 70 (7 x 10) contains ideas of *fulness* (7) and of finite *completeness* (10) (p. 10). It has to do with the *fulness of the Gentiles* taking the fulness of the gospel to the natural branches of the house of Israel and uniting them again under gospel covenants (1 Ne. 15:13; 3 Ne. 16:4; 21:26-27) to save them from spiritual famine (Amos 8:11-12). Paul said "that blindness in part is happened to Israel, until the fulness of the Gentiles be come in" (Rom. 11:25). Jesus taught Peter to forgive his brother fully, not only 7 times, but 7 times 70 (Matt. 18:21-22), a symbolic reference to the *full* forgiveness and ultimate reunification of the *house of Israel.*

Sixty-six *years* is 1 x 2 x 33 years. Interestingly, 33 *years* after religious freedom was established in America, the Father and the Son appeared to the latter-day Joseph of whom Joseph of old spoke and restored the kingdom; also, 66 *years* after religious freedom was established the cornerstones of the temple which Isaiah saw in the top of the mountains were laid (Is. 2:2). By accepting the *restoration* and the sequential message invoked thereby, the 70 may be reconciled to the Father and the Son and be saved from the latter-day famine as implied by 70 written as 1 x 2 x 3.5 x 10.

Seventy *years* reference the *reuniting* of Judah with Ephraim through the fulness of the Gentiles. Seventy *years* after Joseph Smith saw the Son of Man, the Son of Man began to turn back his face toward the natural remnants of Israel (Lev. 26:18; D&C 130:15; HC 5:336). The Jews (66) who would not flee to Jerusalem (D&C 133:13) would suffer from a man held captive by Satan's great chain (6), who John referred to in his 1260-year cornerstone by 666 (Rev. 13:18).

Joseph Smith, Jr.
The seer spoken of by Joseph of old (2 Ne. 3:6, 15) is Joseph Smith, Jr., who was born on Monday, AD 23

December 1805 (JS-H 1:3). For millennia the Lord watched over the seed from which Joseph sprang (cf. Abr. 2:8-9), for he was foreordained to receive the Priesthood and the ministry in the latter-days.

> "Wherefore, meaning the church, thou shalt give heed unto all his words and commandments which he shall give unto you as he receiveth them,... For his word ye shall receive, as if from mine own mouth..." (D&C 21:4-6; cf. 5:9-10).

Malachi spoke of Joseph Smith in the same terms as he spoke of John the Baptist (Mal. 3:1), for they had like missions to prepare the way of the Lord's coming.

**The Chief Cornerstone Reveals the Year
  of Joseph Smith's Birth**
Joseph Smith represents the Firstborn in our dispensation (cf. Ex. 4:22). He is represented in the bottom left-hand sub-cornerstone of Diagram 4.1:

Joseph Smith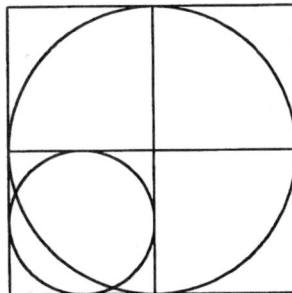

0, 1260 units

Diagram 4.1

Joseph Smith taught "the reality and the divinity of the Lord Jesus Christ as the Son of God" (Gordon B. Hinckley, *Faith, the Essence of True Religion* [Salt Lake City: Deseret Book, 1989], p. 12). Through Joseph Smith the Lord set his hand again the *second time* to *recover* his people (Is. 11:11). An equation for determining Joseph Smith's birth year is thus two times the sum of the radius of the 630-year circle in the Joseph Smith sub-cornerstone and the lines forming the square of that sub-cornerstone (Diagram 4.1):

$$06/04/01 \text{ BC} + 2 \times (9R_{630} \text{ years})$$

$$= \text{AD } 1805_{\text{JS's birthyear}} \tag{1}$$

Two times the 630-*year* circle invokes the entire message of Jesus' 1260-*day* ministry and conveys the idea of *restoration*. The 9R symbolizes birth on earth, and as 1R + 8R it denotes coming from God's presence and rebirth into his kingdom on earth. Since the 630-*year* sub-cornerstone is equivalent to the center 630-*year* cornerstone shown in Diagram 2.3, a message is conveyed that through Joseph Smith the everlasting covenants and the sealing power of the Holy Spirit of Promise would be *restored* to the *earth*. These covenants are the means whereby the faithful sons and daughters of God may be added upon forever and ever in eternity (Abr. 3:26).

The Lord promised that he would remember the covenants made with the fathers, and that in the latter-day he would set his hand again the second time to recover his people (Is. 11:11; 2 Ne. 29:1).

The Relationship of the Discovery of America by Columbus to the Restoration
In 1 Nephi 13:12-19 we read:

> I looked and beheld a man among the Gentiles, who was separated from the seed of my brethren by the many waters; and I beheld the Spirit of God, that it came down and wrought upon the man; and he went forth upon the many waters, even unto the seed of my brethren, who were in the promised land. And it came to pass that I beheld the Spirit of God, that it wrought upon other Gentiles; and they went forth out of captivity, upon the many waters. And it came to pass that I beheld many multitudes of the Gentiles upon the land of promise; I beheld the wrath of God, that it was upon the seed of my brethren; and they were scattered before the Gentiles and were smitten. And I beheld the Spirit of the Lord, that it was upon the Gentiles, and they did prosper and obtain the land for their inheritance;...And I beheld that the power of God was with them... And I, Nephi, beheld that the Gentiles that had gone out of captivity were delivered by the power of God out of the hands of all other nations.

Columbus was the man among the Gentiles who discovered America in AD 1492. Joseph Smith's birth year is related to that year using the pattern shown in the previous chapter for determining Jesus' birth year from the beginning of Israel's regal kingdom. In two dimensions, consider the following from Diagram 4.2: If we add the sum of the radius of the 720-year circle (R_{720} years) and the height of the triangle corresponding to the 720-year circle (R_{720} years/tan 30°) to the year America was discovered by Columbus (AD 1492), we come to AD 1805, the year of Joseph Smith's birth. The 720-year circle is the third circle out from the center in Diagram 4.2. The 720 years correlate with the remnant who are left from Assyria (Is. 11:11).

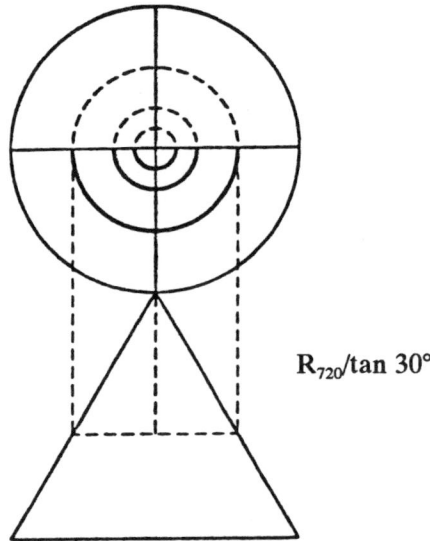

$R_{720}/\tan 30°$

0, 1260 years

Diagram 4.2

The year AD 1492 is also found if we take the 1750 years used in Diagram 2.2 to find the year of the First Vision and break it down into components which fit Daniel's "time and times and the dividing of a time". The components would be 500 years, 1000 years, and 250 years, respectively. If the sum of 250 years and 1260 360-day years are added to Jesus' birth year, the result is AD 1492. This implies that the discovery of America is a key event pertaining to the restoration of the Church through Joseph Smith, since Jesus Christ is the God of this land (Eth. 2:12), and since 1260 years relates to Joseph Smith's birth year as shown in Diagrams 1.1 and 4.1, and since Jesus redeemed the land.

The approximate time of Columbus' discovery of America is also found in the tree of life symbol using the date of Noah's Flood as the reference point. If we expand Diagram 4.2 *sevenfold*, and then add to the reference point the sum of the radius of the outer circle (R_{8820} years) and the height of the corresponding triangle (R_{8820} years/tan 30°), we have AD 1490. Directed by the Spirit Columbus *rediscovered* the land where Adam and the patriarchs, including Noah, dwelt prior to the Flood, and the land to which they will return in the latter-days (D&C 107:53; 116).

Beginning with Jesus' death (the separation of spirit and body), if 500 years (the "time" noted above) are added to the 1260 360-day years, the result is AD 1776, the year of the separation of the United States from Great Britain by the Declaration of Independence (1 Ne. 13:17-19). The 33 years from the time of the establishment of the divinely inspired Constitution guaranteeing religious freedom (AD 1787) to the year of the First Vision (AD 1820) represents the life span of him who inspired the law (D&C 98:4-8; 101:77-80). The rediscovery of America is clearly tied directly to the restoration of the latter-day kingdom.[1] The Lord said to Israel: "I will *lift up mine hand* to the Gentiles...and they shall bring thy sons in their arms, and thy daughters...upon their shoulders" (Is. 49:22).

---

[1]Mark E. Petersen, *The Great Prologue* [Salt Lake City: Deseret Book Company, 1975], p. 24.

Chapter 5

FIRST VISION

> "It was on the morning of a beautiful, clear day, early in the spring of eighteen hundred and twenty.... I saw a pillar of light exactly over my head, above the brightness of the sun, which descended gradually until it fell upon me.... When the light rested upon me I saw two Personages, whose brightness and glory defy all description, standing above me in the air. One of them spake unto me, calling me by name and said, pointing to the other—*This is My Beloved Son. Hear Him*!".
> (JS-H 1:14-17.)

The year of the First Vision is shown in the symbolism associated with the 3 hours of darkness "over all the land" on crucifixion day using the year of the abomination of desolation of the temple in Jerusalem by the Romans (AD 70) as the reference point (chapter two). This was the temple to which the Jews thought Jesus referred when he gave them the sign (authority) by which he cleansed the temple (John 2:19-21). Using the year that the divinely inspired Constitution of the United States was established as the reference point, the year of the First Vision was also pointed to by the number of years in the mortal life of him who inspired the law (chapter four).

Although Joseph Smith did not give a specific day when the First Vision occurred "early in the spring of eighteen hundred and twenty", a Sunday would certainly have been an appropriate day from both a practical and a symbolic viewpoint. On a Sunday morning it might have been easier to find a solitary place than on a work day; and with the First Vision the light began to break forth among them who had been sitting in darkness for centuries (D&C 45:28).

The Face of the Son of Man
Joseph Smith was told that if he lived until he was 85 *years* old, he would see the face of the Son of Man (D&C 130:15). That would have been sometime in Joseph's 86th *year*. Following the pattern used to teach Abraham the age of accountability (p. 3), Joseph Smith probably saw the face of the Son of Man 86 *days* from 1 January 1820 on the Julian calendar, for that day celebrates revival to the Romans. The Romans destroyed Jerusalem and its temple in the abomination of desolation, and that symbolism points to the First Vision (pp. 21-23). The Julian calendar was established in 46 BC. (Webster's Third New International Dictionary, "Julian Calendar"; also see *Reexploring the Book of Mormon*, F.A.R.M.S., 1992, p. 210.)

$$01/01/1820 \text{ AD} + 86 \text{ days} = 26/03/1820 \quad (2)$$

Sunday, AD 26 March 1820, is the probable date of the First Vision. The 1260-day cornerstone seems to confirm this date.

The First Vision From the Chief Cornerstone
Revelation (First Vision) is the second cornerstone of the restored kingdom (the sub-cornerstone in the top left-hand quadrant of Diagram 5.1 below). The circle in the inner square has a circumference of 630 days, the same as the circle in the First Vision sub-cornerstone. The height of the Alpha sign which forms a compass pointing up to God for light and knowledge is 86 days. These 86 days seem to correlate with the 86 days noted

above showing Sunday, AD 26 March 1820, as the most probable date for the First Vision.

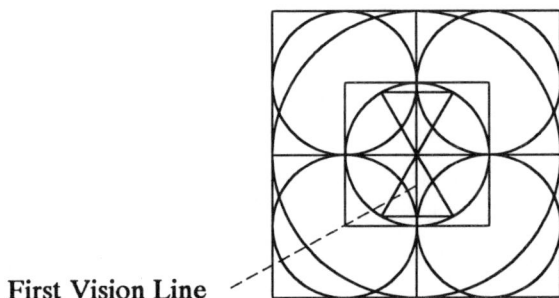

First Vision Line

1260 days

Diagram 5.1

The 86 days are also along the faith line of the cruciform (which invokes the gospel *merism*). It was by faith in the word of God written by James the Apostle that Joseph Smith resolved to pray. Joseph wrote:

> "I was one day reading the Epistle of James, first chapter and fifth verse, which reads: *If any of you lack wisdom, let him ask of God, that giveth to all men liberally, and upbraideth not; and it shall be given him.* Never did any passage of scripture come with more power to the heart of man than this did at this time to mine. It seemed to enter with great force into every feeling of my heart. I reflected on it again and again, knowing that if any person needed wisdom from God, I did;... At length I came to the conclusion that I must either remain in darkness and confusion, or else I must do as James directs, that is, ask of God. I at length came to the determination to "ask of God,"

concluding that if he gave wisdom to them that lacked wisdom, and would give liberally, and not upbraid, I might venture. So, in accordance with this, my determination to ask of God, I retired to the woods to make the attempt."
(JS-H 1:11-14).

"Joseph's humble prayer was answered, and he listened to the Lord" (LDS Hymn No. 26), for God said, "This is my Beloved Son. Hear Him" (JS-H 1:17)!

The First Vision and the Melchizedek Priesthood
The First Vision line in Diagram 5.1 is 86 days, and the short line connecting the base of the triangle to the center point of the bottom line of the inner square is 14 days. The sum of the 86-day line and the 14-day line equals 100 days, the radius of the 630-day circle. This is another confirmation of Sunday, AD 26 March 1820, as the most probable day for the First Vision. This is because the number 14 relates to the Melchizedek Priesthood, and the Melchizedek Priesthood is necessary to see God. Without the ordinances and authority of the Melchizedek Priesthood the power of godliness is not manifest to men in the flesh. Without this no man can see the face of God and live (D&C 84:21-22; cf. JST Ex. 34). Joseph Fielding Smith explained why Joseph Smith was able to commune with God, face to face, before the Melchizedek Priesthood was restored (*Doctrines of Salvation* 1:4; Ez. 20:35).

If the 86 days noted above are *determinative* as well as *representative* as regards the date of the First Vision, then so might be the 14 days as regards the date when the Melchizedek Priesthood was restored.

The 14-day line suggests that the Melchizedek Priesthood and its appendage, the Aaronic Priesthood, were received 14 days apart. This will be explored in a subsequent chapter.

Joseph Smith's Birthday From the First Vision
The day of Joseph Smith's birth in AD 1805 can be found using 26 March as the reference point in AD 1805 to equate the person of Joseph Smith, Jr., with him who received the First Vision. The inscribed circle in the center square of Diagram 5.1 has a circumference of 630 days. This is equivalent to the circle in the Joseph Smith sub-cornerstone (Diagram 4.1) when *days* are used as the unit of measure. Using two dimensions and following the pattern shown in Diagram 4.2, if we add the sum of the radius of the 630-day circle (R_{630} days) and the height of the triangle (R_{630} days/tan 30°) to 26 March, we obtain the following:

$$26/03/1805 \text{ AD} + (R_{630} \text{ days} + R_{630} \text{ days/tan } 30°)$$

$$= 23/12/1805 \text{ AD} \qquad (1.1)$$

This correlation also serves to confirm Sunday, AD 26 March 1820, as the most likely date for the First Vision.

YHWH (Jehovah) + Alpha and Omega = 2520 Years
The English rendering of YHWH (Jehovah) and Alpha and Omega can be seen in the center square of Diagram 5.1. When years are used as the unit of measure, the sum YHWH + Alpha ($\wedge$) and Omega (Ω) equals 2520 years (see also pp. 84-86):

Y = (100.2 + 100.2 + 86.6) years = 287 years
H = (200.5 + 100.2 + 200.5) years = 501.2 years
W = (157.5 + 100.2 + 100.2 + 157.5) years = 515.4 years
H = (200.5 + 100.2 + 200.5) years = 501.2 years

$\wedge$ = (100.2 + 100.2) years = 200.4 years
Ω = (100.2 + 315 + 100.2) years = 515.4 years

As noted above Joseph Smith was told that if he lived until then, he would see the face of the Son of Man in his 86th year. Anciently, the Son of Man set his face against Israel because of disobedience and initiated a *seven times* punishment period as warned (Lev. 26:17-18). In one of his conference talks, Joseph Smith suggested that in AD 1890 a *seven times* period (7 x 360 *years* = 2520 *years*) would come to an end, and the Son of Man would *turn back* his face toward Israel. In referring to the 2520 years, Joseph Smith said:

> "Then read the 14th chapter of Revelation, 6th and 7th verses... And Hosea, 6th chapter, After two days [will he revive us: in the third day he will raise us up], etc.,— 2520 years; which brings it to 1890. The coming of the Son of Man never will be—never can be till the judgments spoken of for this hour are poured out" (HC 5:336).

The flaming sword turns every way to keep the way of the tree of life (Moses 4:31). The 86 years and the 360 years noted above are seen in the Omega sign associated with the 720-year circle in the tree of life symbol shown in Diagram 5.2. The 86-year lines extend from the 1260-year circle to the 720-year circle. There were 720 years from the time the Northern Kingdom of Israel was taken captive by Assyria in 721 BC to the birth of Christ in 1 BC. In the dispensation of the fulness of times, the Lord would set his hand again the second time to *recover* the remnant left from Assyria, and the dispersed of Judah, and *restore* the Ten Tribes (Is. 11:11-12; A of F 1:10). A semicircle of the 720-year circle which connects with the 86-year lines to form an Omega sign equals 360 years. The 360 *years* correlate with the 360 *days* of the *Omega year* of Jesus' life and ministry; also, 7 x 360 years equals the 2520 years noted above. The Alpha sign is formed by the two upward-pointing sides of the triangle. It represents a mountain where light and truth are revealed from God to man on earth. The length of one line of the Alpha sign plus the radius of the 1260-year circle gives the length of the flaming sword (p. 123: Diagram 14.3).

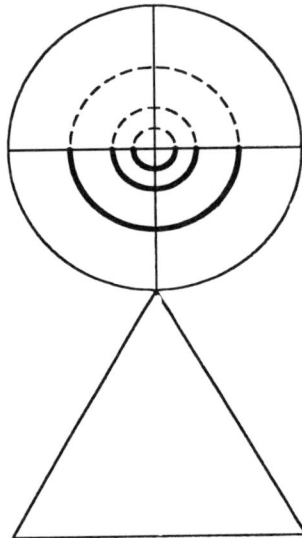

0, 1260 years

Diagram 5.2

The sum of an Alpha and Omega sign in the 1260-year tree of life symbol using the 720-year circle shown in Diagram 5.2 equals 1335 *years*. This correlates with the 1335 *days* noted by Daniel (Dan. 12:12) and shows how leadership succession would occur in the restored Church (pp. 90-91). Using the 360-year circle the Alpha and Omega sign equals 1096 years, thus giving the number of years from the establishment of Israel's regal kingdom to the birth of Christ (p. 34).

The Year AD 1890
It appears that AD 1890 began a transition period as regards the Jews (Lev. 26:17-18; D&C 19:27; HC 5:336). It ended a 2520-year period regarding them, and it was 70 years after the First Vision. The pouring out of judgments upon the nations would prepare the way for their reunification with Ephraim (pp. 36-38; cf. Gen. 46:26-27). The Son of Man would begin to *turn back* his face (presence) toward the natural remnants in that they would begin to receive the gospel and the Melchizedek Priesthood; and the nations in which they dwell would see a sharp two-edged sword coming out of his mouth, symbolic of the word of God (Rev. 1:16; D&C 6:1-4); they would see his eyes as a flame of fire, symbolic of the justice of God, if they would not open their doors for the preaching of the gospel to all the house of Israel (Rev. 1:14; 14:6; 1 Ne. 15:30; 2 Ne. 25:22; HC 5:336); they would hear his voice as the sound of many waters—peoples and multitudes gathering together (Rev. 1:15; 17:15); and finally they would see his arm made bare in bringing the gospel to Israel (Is. 52:9-10; Rev. 1:16; 11:6, 11-13; 1 Ne. 22:10-11; D&C 1:14; 35:13-14; 45:44-48; 88:93; JS-M 1:26, 33-36).

All kindreds of the earth would be blessed with the blessings of the gospel through the seed of Abraham (the Priesthood); and the house of Israel would be brought out of captivity and gathered to the lands of their inheritance, and they would know that the Lord is their Savior and Redeemer (1 Ne. 22:12); and they would see his feet upon the mountains, even of him who is the founder of peace, the Lord who has redeemed his people, and how beautiful they would be (Mosiah 15:18).

The year AD 1890 marked the end of the physical battles between native Americans and the Gentiles from Europe, and the continued rise of a great nation among the Gentiles, "even upon the face of this land" (1 Ne. 22:7-9). It was the year Wilford Woodruff issued the *Manifesto* (OD—1) and the year that a major restructuring of the political system in Europe began to take place which led to world war and the opening of the doors of the nations to hear the gospel. In AD 1893 the mountain of the Lord's house was established in the top of the mountains and all nations began to flow unto it as Isaiah foresaw (Is. 2:2). Over seventeen million people came from Europe to America through Ellis Island from 1890 to 1924; the remnant who fled to Zion and to Palestine were spared the holocaust of World War II caused by the 666 referred to by John in the 1260-year cornerstone (JST Rev. 12:5; 13:18).

"Awake and arise and go forth to meet the Bridegroom; behold...the Bridegroom cometh; go ye out to meet him. Prepare yourselves for the great day of the Lord.... Let them...who are among the Gentiles flee unto Zion. And let them who be of

Judah flee unto Jerusalem, unto the mountains of the Lord's house." (D&C 133:10-13.)

Temples are mountains to which the house of Israel should flee in the last days. After the Jews have gathered to Jerusalem and begun to receive the gospel, they will build a temple there as directed by the First Presidency in preparation for the coming of their King.

"How beautiful upon the mountains are the feet of him that bringeth good tidings, that publisheth peace; that bringeth good tidings of good, that publisheth salvation; that saith unto Zion, Thy God reigneth" (Is. 52:7)!

The number 666 in the 1260-*year* cornerstone relates to the means provided for Judah (66) to reunite with Ephraim in order to be freed from Satan's great chain (6) and to find refuge from 666 (pp. 99-101, 106).

The First Vision and the Salt Lake Temple
The cornerstones of the Salt Lake Temple were laid on AD 6 April 1853, 33 years after the First Vision, reminiscent of Jesus' 33-year life (*Ensign*, March 1993, p. 18); thirty-nine years later, again on Jesus' birthday, the capstone was set, reminiscent of the 39-year life of Jesus' latter-day messenger (Mal. 3:1; D&C 135:1); and 40 years from the time the cornerstones were laid, the temple was dedicated, reminiscent of the 40 years during which the children of Israel wandered in the wilderness prior to entering the promised land. Joseph Smith was a modern-day Moses (2 Ne. 3:9), and his successors have been leading latter-day Israel from this temple in the mountains ever since.

Chapter 6

COMING FORTH OF THE BOOK OF MORMON

> "At length the time arrived for obtaining the
> plates, the Urim and Thummim, and the breast-
> plate. On the twenty-second day of September,
> one thousand eight hundred and twenty-seven,
> having gone as usual at the end of another year to
> the place where they were deposited, the same
> heavenly messenger delivered them up to me..."
> (JS-H 1:59).

The Book of Mormon was received by the mercy (gift)
and power of God (D&C 1:29; 135:3; Testimony of the
Three Witnesses). It is the stick of Ephraim referred
to by Ezekiel (Ez. 37:16). It is God's new covenant
(D&C 84:57). Moroni, the last of the Book of Mormon
prophets, holds the keys of the record of the stick of
Ephraim (D&C 27:5) which contains the fulness of the
gospel of Jesus Christ to the Gentiles and also to the
Jews (D&C 20:9; 35:17).

Ezekiel prophesied that the stick of Ephraim and
the stick of Judah would be joined and the two would
be one in the hand of the Lord (Ez. 37:19). In bringing
these two records together the Lord would begin to
recover his people. The stick of Ephraim came forth
through Joseph Smith. His mortal mission was related
to the mortal mission of John the Baptist. Both were
forerunners of the Lord to prepare the way for his
coming and both were referred to in the same verse in
Malachi's[1] prophetic declaration along with the everlasting covenant which the Lord sends into the world to
be a light to the world and a standard for his people.

---

[1]Malachi means *my messenger.*

"Behold, I will send my messenger, and he shall prepare the way before me" (Mal. 3:1; cf. Mark 1:2-4; JS-H 1:36).

"...I have sent mine everlasting covenant into the world...to be a messenger before my face to prepare the way before me" (D&C 45:9).

Both John the Baptist and Joseph Smith had similar experiences with all three members of the Godhead. After John baptized the Lamb of God, he testified that the Spirit of God descended like a dove and lighted upon Jesus, and the Father said: "This is my beloved Son, in whom I am well pleased. Hear ye him" (JST Matt. 3:45-46). After Joseph Smith was quickened by the Spirit and saw the Father and the Son, he testified: "One of them spake unto me, calling me by name and said, pointing to the other—This is My Beloved Son. Hear Him" (JS-H 1:14-17).

John the Baptist returned on Friday, AD 15 May 1829, and in the name of the Messiah conferred upon Joseph Smith and Oliver Cowdery the Priesthood of Aaron, which holds the keys of the ministering of angels, and of the gospel of repentance, and of baptism by immersion for the remission of sins (D&C 13).

The First Coming of Moroni
From the Chief Cornerstone

The date of Moroni's first coming to Joseph Smith to reveal the record of the stick of Ephraim and also the date that Joseph Smith received the record four years later were set in the chief cornerstone. After relating certain events subsequent to the First Vision, Joseph

Smith described the following setting for his prayer on the eve of Moroni's first visit:

> "...I often felt condemned for my weakness and imperfections; when, on the evening of the above-mentioned twenty-first of September, after I had retired to bed for the night, I betook myself to prayer and supplication to Almighty God for forgiveness of all my sins and follies, and also for a manifestation to me, that I might know of my state and standing before him; for I had full confidence in obtaining a divine manifestation, as I previously had one" (JS-H 1:29).

Sometime after Joseph Smith went to bed Sunday night, AD 21 September 1823, Moroni appeared to him. Joseph recorded:

> "He called me by name, and said unto me that he was a messenger sent from the presence of God to me, and that his name was Moroni" (JS-H 1:33).

Using the 1260-day cornerstone and the above information, a simple equation can be formulated showing the date of Moroni's first visit (Diagram 6.1):

The first term in the equation is the reference point—Joseph Smith's birthday, Monday, AD 23 December 1805 (JS-H 1:3), the year of which was set in the 1260-year cornerstone (pp. 14-15).

A second term references the restoration of the teachings of Jesus' 1260-day ministry which are contained in the stick of Ephraim and in the stick of Judah. Therefore, one round of the 1260-day circle in the chief cornerstone is added.

The Aaronic Priesthood holds the keys of the gospel of repentance and of baptism. Since John the Baptist held these keys, a third term referencing John the Baptist is used. This term is the number of days from his birthday to Jesus' birthday—six months or 183 days (Luke 1:24-57).

A fourth term is used to show that through the gospel contained in the Book of Mormon, namely, faith in Jesus Christ, repentance, and baptism, the Lord would recover his people again the second time from the *four quarters of the earth* (Is. 11:11-12; 3 Ne. 21:1-7; 27:19-22). This term is thus found by using the 630-day circle in the Revelation sub-cornerstone and multiplying it by 8 to indicate rebirth. Eight is also four times two, showing the *geographical completeness* of the recovery of the Lord's people, and that it is the *second time*.

Revelation

Joseph Smith

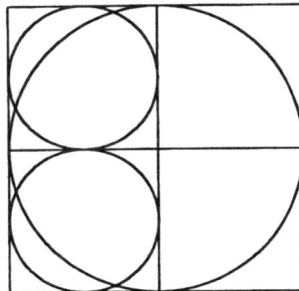

0, 1260 days

Diagram 6.1

The four terms give the following equation:

$23/12/1805_{\text{JS' birthday}}$

$+ 1260 \text{ days} + 183 \text{ days} + 5040 \text{ days}$

$= 22/09/1823_{\text{Moroni}}$ (3)

Sometime after Joseph Smith prayed and went to bed Sunday night, AD 21 September 1823, Moroni appeared to Joseph and stayed with him the morning of Monday, AD 22 September 1823. According to Joseph Smith's testimony, this is what happened:

> "During the space of time which intervened between the time I had the vision and the year eighteen hundred and twenty-three...I was left to all kinds of temptations...

> "In consequence of these things, I often felt condemned for my weakness and imperfections; when, on the evening of the above mentioned twenty-first of September, after I had retired to my bed for the night, I betook myself to prayer and supplication to Almighty God for forgiveness of all my sins and follies, and also for a manifestation to me, that I might know of my state and standing before him; for I had full confidence in obtaining a divine manifestation, as I previously had one. While I was thus in the act of calling upon God, I discovered a light appearing in my room, which continued to increase until the room was lighter than at noonday, when immediately a personage appeared at my bedside, standing in the air, for his feet did not touch the floor.... He called me by name, and said unto me that he was a messenger sent from the presence of God to me, and that his name was Moroni; that God had

a work for me to do;... He said there was a book deposited, written upon gold plates, giving an account of the former inhabitants of this continent..." (JS-H 1:28-34).

The First Coming of Moroni
From the Tree of Life Symbol

Another way of showing the date of Moroni's first visit to Joseph Smith is to use the tree of life symbol. Joseph Smith was the rod which came forth out of the Stem of Jesse to recover the remnant left from Assyria:

> "And there shall come forth a rod out of the stem of Jesse, and a Branch shall grow out of his roots... And it shall come to pass in that day, that the Lord shall set his hand again the second time to recover the remnant of his people, which shall be left, from Assyria..." (Is. 11:1, 11).

> "What is the rod spoken of in the first verse of the 11th chapter of Isaiah, that should come of the Stem of Jesse? Behold, saith the Lord: It is a servant in the hands of Christ, who is partly a descendant of Jesse as well as of Ephraim, or of the house of Joseph, on whom there is laid much power" (D&C 113:3-4).

The first term in an equation using the tree of life symbol is the birthday of the rod which came forth out of the Stem of Jesse. The second term relates to his mission to recover the remnant of the Lord's people which are left from Assyria. The Ten Tribes were taken captive by Assyria in 721 BC or 720 *years* before the birth of Christ. They would be *recovered* in the dispensation of the fulness of times. Therefore, the second term is 7 x 720 *days* = 5040 *days*.

> "After two days will he revive us and in the third
> day he will raise us up, and we shall live in his
> sight" (Hosea 6:2).

The rod came out of the Stem of Jesse in the Lord's
3rd day from the time Israel was taken captive by
Assyria as well as from the time Judah was taken
captive by Babylon. Therefore, the third term in this
equation is 3 days. The Stem of Jesse is along the
vertical line extending down from the center of the
concentric circles in Diagram 6.2.

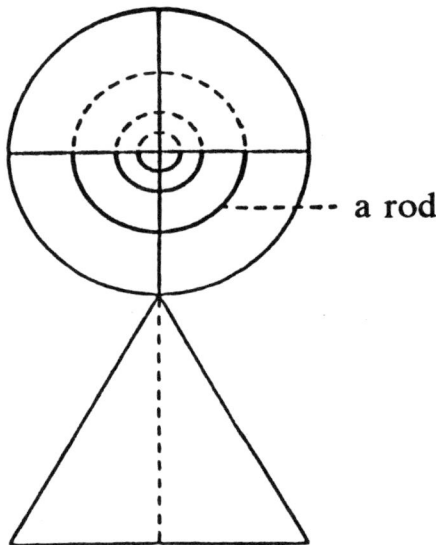

0, 1260 days

Diagram 6.2

A rod coming out of the Stem of Jesse at the 720-day circle point might be visualized by a quarter arc of the 720-day circle or 180 days (πR_{720} days/4). Thus, the fourth term is 180 days. The gospel contained in the Book of Mormon is the means of recovering the remnant left from Assyria. Therefore, the fifth term is 1260 days to reference Jesus' 1260-day gospel ministry. Combining these terms gives the following equation:

$$23/12/1805_{\text{JS' birthday}} + 5040 \text{ days} + 3 \text{ days}$$

$$+ 180 \text{ days} + 1260 \text{ days}$$

$$= 22/09/1823_{\text{Moroni}} \qquad (3.1)$$

The 5040-day term in equation (3.1) is also seen by considering the Church in terms of a seven candlestick symbol consisting of semicircles. Semicircles are represented by πR, where π is a constant with a value of 3.1416... and R is the radius of a semicircle (or circle). The Church is meaningful because of the Atonement and Resurrection; thus, in this case $R = R_{360}$, and $\pi R = \pi R_{360}$. The πR_{360} is multiplied by 28 days (2 x 14 days) to yield 5040 days because the Son of God was the Paschal Lamb on the 14th day of Abib.

John the Baptist's Birthday
The fact that a 183-day period is necessary in equations 3.0 and 3.1 to calculate the date of Moroni's first appearance to Joseph Smith implies that John the Baptist was born on Sunday, 6 October 2 BC, Sunday being the first day of the Hebrew week. This is 183 days before Christ's birth on Thursday, 6 April 1 BC.

Moroni's First Coming From the First Vision
Returning to Hosea's statement that "in the [Lord's] third day he will raise us up" and to the rod coming out of the Stem of Jesse (180 days) (pp. 60-61), if we add 3 *years* and 180 *days* (half a time), we have 1275 days. Counting (inclusively) 1275 days from the calculated date of the First Vision (Sunday, AD 26 March 1820), we come to Sunday, AD 21 September 1823; and 70 years from AD 1823 brings us to AD 1893 and the Salt Lake Temple with all the implications heretofore referred to regarding careful preparations for the reunification of the house of Israel. (D&C 133:12-15; Rev. 14:6; Is. 2:2; Dan. 9:2; Jer. 25:12; HC 5:336.)

Receipt of the Book of Mormon Record
Moroni revealed the third sub-cornerstone of the restoration, namely, Scripture (the Book of Mormon) (top right-hand quadrant of Diagram 6.3).

During the night of 21 September 1823, Moroni appeared to Joseph 3 times, a 4th time the next morning, and a 5th time on the Hill Cumorah later in the day. The 3 times correlate with the Savior's 3 *knocks* in the garden of Gethsemane to enable forgiveness of sins which Joseph prayerfully sought (Matt. 26:39, 42, 44; JS-H 1:29). A 4th time conveys the idea that the name of Joseph Smith should be had for good and evil among all nations, kindreds, and tongues (JS-H 1:33). A 5th time on the Hill Cumorah would be a reminder that Joseph Smith was not to show the plates to any unauthorized person, otherwise he would be cut off or destroyed (JS-H 1:42, 59). The number 5 relates to punishment (Smith's Bible Dictionary, "Number").

On AD 22 September 1823, Joseph Smith traveled to the place on the Hill Cumorah which he saw clearly in his mind while Moroni was telling him about the plates. When Joseph attempted to take the plates, he was forbidden and informed that the time had not yet come, and that he was to return each year for four years on that anniversary until the time should come for obtaining them. The circumference of the 1260-day circle plus its radius equals *four years*. The *restored* Book of Mormon would reach the *whole earth*.

> "[Moroni] told me, that when I got those plates of which he had spoken—for the time that they should be obtained was not yet fulfilled—I should not show them to any person;... if I did I should be destroyed. While he was conversing with me about the plates, the vision was opened to my mind that I could see the place where the plates were deposited, and that so clearly and distinctly that I knew the place again when I visited it.... Convenient to the village of Manchester, Ontario county, New York, stands a hill of considerable size, and the most elevated of any in the neighborhood. On the west side of this hill, not far from the top, under a stone of considerable size, lay the plates, deposited in a stone box. This stone was thick and rounding in the middle on the upper side, and thinner towards the edges, so that the middle part of it was visible above the ground, but the edge all around was covered with earth. Having removed the earth, I obtained a lever, which I got fixed under the edge of the stone, and with a little exertion raised it up. I looked in, and there indeed did I behold the plates, the Urim and Thummim, and the breastplate, as stated by the messenger....

"I made an attempt to take them out, but was forbidden by the messenger, and *was again informed that the time for bringing them forth had not yet arrived, neither would it, until four years from that time;* but he told me that I should come to that place precisely in one year from that time, and that he would there meet with me, and that I should continue to do so until the time should come for obtaining the plates.

"Accordingly, as I had been commanded, I went at the end of each year, and at each time I found the same messenger there, and received instruction and intelligence from him at each of our interviews, respecting what the Lord was going to do, and how and in what manner his kingdom was to be conducted in the last days." (JS-H 1:42-54; italics added.)

Receipt of this *Gospel Record* from an angel from God's presence, seen symbolically as one round of Jesus' 1260-day gospel ministry circle plus its radius R, would be 1461 days (1260 days plus 201 days) after Moroni appeared to Joseph Smith. This is also deduced from Ezekiel's prophecy that in the latter-days the sticks of Ephraim and of Judah would be joined.

"The word of the Lord came again unto me, saying, Moreover, thou son of man, take thee one stick, and write upon it, For Judah, and for the children of Israel his companions: then take another stick, and write upon it, For Joseph, the stick of Ephraim, and for all the house of Israel his companions: And join them one to another into one stick; and they shall be one in thine hand." (Ez. 37:15-17.)

If the Scripture sub-cornerstone (upper right-hand quadrant of Diagram 6.3) is divided by a cruciform, there are four *second level* sub-cornerstones. They might be used to represent the Standard Works that would reach the whole earth. Their inscribed circles have 315-day circumferences with radii of 50.1 days. An equation for the date of the receipt of the Book of Mormon plates would then be as follows: The date of Moroni's first visit with Joseph Smith on the Hill Cumorah + one round of each of the circles in the four Standard Works sub-cornerstones ($4 \times 2\pi R_{315}$ = 1260 days) + one half of the four ties lines of the four sub-cornerstones ($\frac{1}{2} \times 4 \times R_{315}$ = 201 days) = the date of the receipt of the Book of Mormon plates. One half is used because only two of the four Standard Works are being referred to, the sticks of Ephraim and Judah. (Interestingly, *four years* is equal to one round of the 1260-*day circle* plus its *radius*—implying that the *world* through *obedience* to the *restoration* of the *truth* taught in *Jesus' ministry* will bring eternal life in *eternity*.)

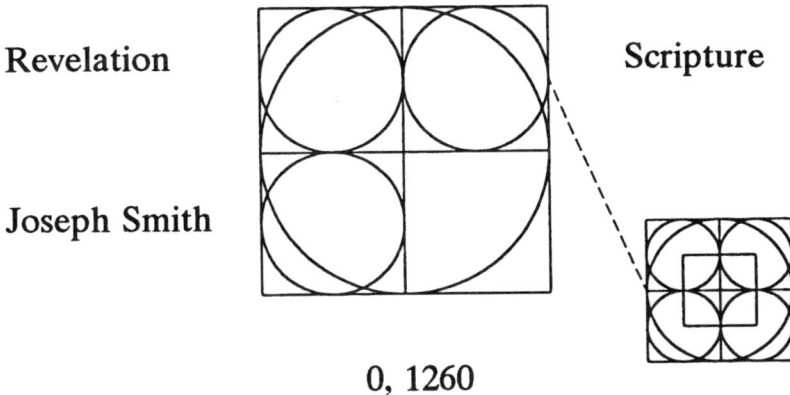

Revelation   Scripture

Joseph Smith

0, 1260

Diagram 6.3

The three terms noted above give the following result:

$$22/09/1823_{\text{Moroni's first visit to Joseph Smith}}$$

$$+ 1260 \text{ days} + 201 \text{ days} = 21/09/1827_{\text{BofM}} \quad (4)$$

On Friday, AD 21 September 1827, the four years were completed. The next day, Saturday, AD 22 September 1827, on the anniversary of Joseph Smith's first visit with Moroni on the Hill Cumorah, Joseph Smith received the Book of Mormon plates. He wrote:

> "At length the time arrived for obtaining the plates, the Urim and Thummim, and the breast-plate. On the twenty-second day of September, one thousand eight hundred and twenty-seven, having gone as usual at the end of another year to the place where they were deposited, the same heavenly messenger delivered them up to me with this charge: that I should be responsible for them; that if I should let them go carelessly, or through any neglect of mine, I should be cut off; but that if I would use all my endeavors to preserve them, until he, the messenger, should call for them, they should be protected." (JS-H 1:59).

History shows that Joseph Smith, with Oliver Cowdery as scribe, accomplished the work of translating the Book of Mormon in 63 days[2] (3^2 x 7 days). This conveys the idea that the Book of Mormon was trans-

---

[2]History of the Church 1:32-33; Richard Lyman Bushman, *Book of Mormon Authorship Revisited*, edited by Noel B. Reynolds [Provo: Foundation for Ancient Research and Mormon Studies, 1997], p. 23.

lated by the *power of Jesus Christ* and that it contains the *fulness* of the gospel. The gospel is the word of God as revealed by the *Spirit of God.* The emphasis is on the power or Spirit of God. *Days* represent *obedience* to the gospel contained in the Book of Mormon which is the means of judging the nations that possess it (2 Ne. 25:22).

Enoch and the Book of Mormon
In the book of Moses we read what the Lord said to Enoch about the restoration and the coming forth of the Book of Mormon:

> "And the day shall come that the earth shall rest, but before that day the heavens shall be darkened, and a veil of darkness shall cover the earth; and the heavens shall shake, and also the earth; and great tribulations shall be among the children of men, but my people will I preserve;

> "And righteousness will I send down out of heaven; and truth will I send forth out of the earth, to bear testimony of mine Only Begotten; his resurrection from the dead; yea, and also the resurrection of all men; and righteousness and truth will I cause to sweep the earth as with a flood, to gather out mine elect from the four quarters of the earth, unto a place which I shall prepare, an Holy City, that my people may gird up their loins, and be looking forth for the time of my coming" (Moses 7:61-62).

The Book of Mormon as the New Covenant
In the great revelation on the Priesthood (D&C 84), the Lord referred to the Book of Mormon as the "new

covenant" and warned that unless we remember to do according to that which is written, we will be under condemnation (D&C 84:57).

The Book of Mormon and the First Vision
On AD 26 March 1830, 10 years from the probable date of the First Vision (pp. 45-46), the *Wayne Sentinel* announced that the Book of Mormon was available for purchase. One week earlier, on AD 19 March 1830, the *Wayne Sentinel* announced that the Book of Mormon would be available in one week.[3]

The Book of Mormon and the Gathering
in One of All Things
In modern revelation the Lord speaks of the hour when he will come to earth and drink of the fruit of the vine with all those whom the Father has given him out of the world (D&C 27:5-14). Included in that gathering will be Moroni, who holds the keys of the record of the stick of Ephraim, and John the Baptist, who restored the Aaronic Priesthood, and Elijah, who restored the keys of the power of turning the hearts of the children to the fathers, and Abraham, Isaac, Jacob, Joseph, and Michael or Adam, the Ancient of Days, and also Peter, James, and John, unto whom the Lord committed the keys of the kingdom. In the dispensation of the fulness of times, the Lord will gather together in one all things, both which are in heaven, and which are on earth.

---

[3]Egbert B. Grandin was the publisher of the *Wayne Sentinel* in Palmyra, New York (B. H. Roberts, *A Comprehensive History of the Church of Jesus Christ of Latter-day Saints* [Salt Lake City: Deseret News Press, 1930], Vol. I, p. 157).

Chapter 7

RESTORATION OF THE PRIESTHOOD

> "Upon you my fellow servants, in the name of Messiah I confer the Priesthood of Aaron, which holds the keys of the ministering of angels, and of the gospel of repentance, and of baptism by immersion for the remission of sins; and this shall never be taken again from the earth, until the sons of Levi do offer again an offering unto the Lord in righteousness" (D&C 13).

The Aaronic Priesthood holds "the keys...to administer in *outward* ordinances, the letter of the gospel" (D&C 107:20; italics added). It is an appendage to the Melchizedek Priesthood (D&C 107:5, 14, 20) which holds "the keys of all the *spiritual* blessings of the church" (D&C 107:18; italics added).

The Restoration of the Aaronic Priesthood From the Chief Cornerstone

The Priesthood keys and authority held by the Apostles and Prophets constitute the fourth sub-cornerstone of the restoration (bottom right-hand quadrant of Diagram 7.1).

To show that the date of the Aaronic Priesthood restoration by John the Baptist was also set in the 1260-day cornerstone, consider the following information: First, John the Baptist was born six months (183 days) before Jesus Christ (Luke 1:24-57). Second, the Lord told ancient Israel that if they were disobedient and did not repent, he would punish them *seven times* (7 x 360 years = 2520 years) and bring a sword upon them (Lev. 26:18, 25). But if thereafter they would confess their iniquity and repent, the Lord would *restore* to them the covenants he made with their fathers (Lev. 26:40-42). A term of 2520 *days* would be a reminder of the need for obedience just as the circumcision of male children when they were 8 *days* old was a reminder that children are not accountable before God until they are 8 *years* old (JST Gen. 17:11). A term of 802 days would be a reminder of the sword of truth (Eph. 6:17). In the 1260-day tree of life symbol, the length of the sword of truth is 802 days (p. 123, Diagram 14.3). The gospel is the word of the Lord and the word of the Lord is truth (D&C 84:45). This is shown numerically by the fact that the lines of the cruciform in Diagram 7.1, which represent the first principles and ordinances of the gospel, also equal 802 days (4 x R_{1260}); and the gospel (the sword of truth) is the means of judging the nations (2 Ne. 22:25; 29:11; 33:15).

Revelation 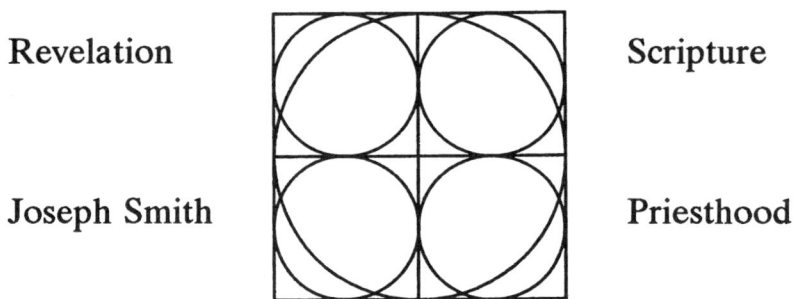 Scripture

Joseph Smith   Priesthood

0, 1260 days

Diagram 7.1

Next, the Apostles, represented by 12, hold the keys of Priesthood power and authority (3 x 14) to perform (complete) saving ordinances (10). The product 12 x 3 x 14 x 10 days = 5040 days. This also equals 8 times the 630-day circle in the Priesthood sub-cornerstone. This conveys a message that through the Aaronic Priesthood ordinance of baptism all kindreds of the earth may be born into the kingdom of God by water (John 3:5; JST Matt. 5:4).

Considering the above information, an equation for the restoration of the Aaronic Priesthood might be written as follows:

$$23/12/1805_{\text{JS's birthday}}$$

$$+\ 183\ \text{days}_{\text{JB's birthday-JC's birthday}}$$

$$+\ 2520\ \text{days}_{\text{reminder of Israel's seven times punishment}}$$

$$+\ 802\ \text{days}_{\text{reminder of sword of truth}}$$

$$+\ 5040\ \text{days}_{\text{reminder of Priesthood ordinance of baptism}}$$

$$=\ 15/05/1829_{\text{AP}} \qquad (5)$$

On Friday, AD 15 May 1829, John the Baptist returned and conferred upon Joseph Smith and Oliver Cowdery the keys and the power and authority of the Aaronic Priesthood (D&C 13; JS-H 1:72).

The Restoration of the Melchizedek Priesthood
  From the Chief Cornerstone
With the restoration of the Aaronic Priesthood, the lines forming an inner square of the chief cornerstone may now be drawn through the centers of the circles in

the sub-cornerstones (Diagram 7.2). Let these lines represent "the words or covenants of eternal life" (p. 25).

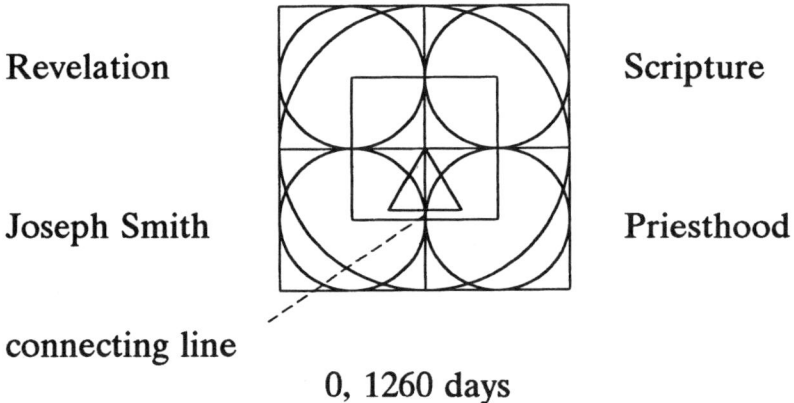

Revelation   Scripture

Joseph Smith   Priesthood

connecting line

0, 1260 days

Diagram 7.2

Jesus' descent from Abraham through King David is 3 x 14 generations. The number 3 relates to the *power of godliness* and in the ordinances of the Melchizedek Priesthood the power of godliness is manifest (D&C 84:20). The number 14 (7 x 2) represents the *fulness* of the Priesthood after the order of the *Son of God*. Therefore, those who receive the Melchizedek Priesthood and remain faithful are sanctified by the *Spirit* unto the renewing of their bodies. They become the *seed of Abraham* and the *kingdom of God* (pp. 7-8).

Anciently, Moses and the Melchizedek Priesthood were taken out of the midst of Israel because of disobedience and the Aaronic Priesthood continued (D&C 84:24-26). An appropriate reminder of the need for obedience in order to retain the Melchizedek Priesthood would be for the Priesthoods of Aaron and Melchizedek to be received *14 days* apart. A 14-day connecting line is seen in Diagram 7.2. It is the short line going vertically upward from the center of the bottom line of the inner square to the base of the upward-pointing equilateral triangle. This line equals 14 days $[R_{630} \times (1 - \cos 30°)]$. It is rounded up since the 86-day First Vision line to which it connects is rounded down. The total of the two lines must equal 100 days, the radius of the 630-day circle shown in Diagram 5.1. An equation for the probable date when Peter, James, and John restored the Melchizedek Priesthood (D&C 128:20) would then be as follows (counting *inclusively*):

$$15/05/1829_{AP} + 14 \text{ days} = 28/05/1829_{MP} \qquad (6)$$

Thursday, AD 28 May 1829 also appears to be an acceptable date from an historical perspective.

The Melchizedek Priesthood
and Beholding the Face of God
The Melchizedek Priesthood holds the key to the knowledge of God (D&C 84:19), even the power to behold his face (D&C 84:21-23). This is shown diagrammatically by the fact that the short 14-day line connects with the 86-day First Vision line to make up the 100-day radius of the inner circle shown in Diagrams 5.1. The radial line going upward to the center of the circle in Diagram 7.2 is along the faith line of the cruciform. Joseph Smith was prompted to pray to find an answer to his question when he read in the first chapter of James:

"If any of you lack wisdom, let him ask of God, that giveth to all men liberally, and upbraideth not; and it shall be given him. *But let him ask in faith, nothing wavering.* For he that wavereth is like a wave of the sea driven with the wind and tossed." (James 1:5-6; italics added.)

Days as the unit of measure in the 14-day line represent *obedience* or *faithfulness*. Faithfulness is an essential part of the oath and covenant of the Priesthood:

"...whoso is faithful unto the obtaining these two priesthoods of which I have spoken, and the magnifying their calling, are sanctified by the Spirit unto the renewing of their bodies. They become the sons of Moses and of Aaron and the seed of Abraham, and the church and kingdom, and the elect of God. And also all they who receive this priesthood receive me, saith the Lord;...And he that receiveth me receiveth my Father; And he that receiveth my Father receiveth my Father's kingdom; therefore all that my Father hath shall be given unto him." (D&C 84:33-38.)

The Special Witnesses of Jesus Christ

The Apostles are represented in the fourth quadrant of the chief cornerstone in Diagrams 7.1 and 7.2. The numerical relationship $12 = 3 \times 4$ conveys a message that the 12 Apostles are special witnesses of Jesus Christ in all the world (D&C 107:23). When 12 is written as 3×2^2, the message emphasizes that they are witnesses of the *name* of Jesus Christ in all the world.

Chapter 8

ORGANIZATION OF THE CHURCH

"The rise of the Church of Christ in these last days, being one thousand eight hundred and thirty years since the coming of the our Lord and Savior Jesus Christ in the flesh" (D&C 20:1).

The Church receives members through the ordinances of baptism and confirmation (D&C 20:37, 43, 68). Baptism is an *outward* ordinance. The Aaronic Priesthood has power to administer *outward* ordinances and is an appendage to the Melchizedek Priesthood (D&C 107:14). Confirmation is an ordinance performed by someone holding the Melchizedek Priesthood who is properly authorized by someone holding its keys. The Melchizedek Priesthood has power and authority to administer in all spiritual matters (D&C 107:18).

"And again, by way of commandment to the church concerning the manner of baptism—All those who humble themselves before God, and desire to be baptized, and come forth with broken hearts and contrite spirits, and witness before the church that they have truly repented of all their sins, and are willing to take upon them the name of Jesus Christ, having a determination to serve him to the end, and truly manifest by their works that they have received of the Spirit of Christ unto the remission of their sins, shall be received by baptism into his church" (D&C 20:37).

"The duty of the members after they are received by baptism—The elders and priests are to have a sufficient time to expound all things concerning the church of Christ to their understanding, previous to their partaking of the sacrament and being confirmed by the laying on of the hands of

the elders, so that all things may be done in order" (D&C 20:68).

The Organization of the Church
From the Melchizedek Priesthood

The number 14 relates to the fulness of the Melchizedek Priesthood (pp. 6-7, 72). Fourteen-day lines connect the base lines of the two equilateral triangles to the lower and upper lines of the inner square (see Diagram 8.1). The *outward* plane is represented by the upward-pointing equilateral triangle. In the previous chapter the base line of the upward-pointing triangle was connected to the bottom line of the inner square. The base line of the downward-pointing equilateral triangle must now be connected to the top line of the inner square (Diagram 8.1). The downward-pointing equilateral triangle represents the *spiritual* plane, and its 14-day connecting line is along the baptism line of the cruciform.

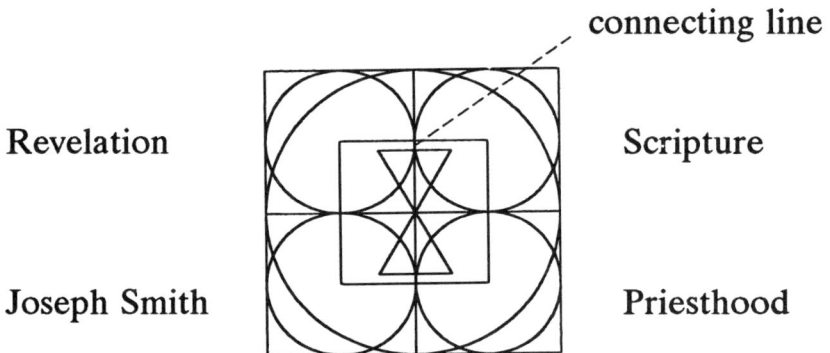

connecting line

Revelation   Scripture

Joseph Smith   Priesthood

0, 1260 days

Diagram 8.1

The date the Church was organized is seen in the 1260-day cornerstone as the sum of the lines forming the equilateral triangle which represents the *outward* plane and the 14-day connecting line to the *spiritual* plane. The sum of the lines forming the upward-pointing triangle is 300 days (3 x R_{630} days). The length of these lines is equivalent to the faith, repentance, and baptism lines of the cruciform in the center square.

A simple equation then for the date the Church was organized from the probable date that the Melchizedek Priesthood was restored is as follows:

$$28/05/1829_{MP}$$

$$+ 300 \text{ days} + 14 \text{ days} = 06/04/1830_{Church} \quad (7)$$

On Tuesday, AD 6 April 1830, The Church of Jesus Christ of Latter-day Saints was organized (D&C 20:1).

The 300 (3 x 10^2) days in equation (7) emphasize that by completing the ordinance of baptism in a faithful manner (D&C 20:37) the gift of the Holy Ghost may be conferred through confirmation (D&C 20:68). It is the Spirit that justifies (perfects) us (Moses 6:60). The 14 days convey a message that confirmation is a Melchizedek Priesthood ordinance, and that by remaining faithful to the end, we shall be *lifted up* at the last day (3 Ne. 27:16, 19-22). The Spirit may be represented by the 9th hour or 3^2 hour line in Diagram 8.1, the *hour* pointing to the death of our Lord and Savior Jesus Christ, and his resurrection on the 3rd day thereafter, counting *inclusively* (p. 13).

The Date of the Restoration of the Church
 From the Date the Aaronic Priesthood was Restored
The date the Church was organized could have been calculated from the date the Aaronic Priesthood was restored (15/05/1829) by adding both 14-day connecting lines to the two triangles in the same operation. Therefore, it is not necessary to know the date the Melchizedek Priesthood was restored to find the date the Church was organized from the chief cornerstone.

YHWH (Jehovah)
With the restoration of the Church, the English rendering of the YHWH sign may now be seen in the center square of Diagram 8.1. Using years as the unit of measure, its numerical value is 1805 years (p. 49). This is the number of years from Jesus' birth to Joseph Smith's birth. The Lord restored his kingdom to earth through Joseph Smith. A message is seen by looking at the individual letters of the YHWH sign. Y pertains to the First Vision; the two back to back H's pertain to "the words or covenants of eternal life;" and W pertains to the house of the Lord as seen in its numerical value of 515 years. There were 515 years from the dedication of the Zerubbabel Temple to Jesus' birth year. With the establishment of the Church upon the chief cornerstone, all the building fitly framed together could now grow "unto an holy temple in the Lord" (Eph. 2:21).

Perfection
The perfection implied by the Savior's invitation to be perfect is to repent, to be baptized, and to keep the commandments, Jesus having set the example (2 Ne. 31:4-10). This enables us to be *justified* (perfected) by

the Spirit (Moses 6:60). The Resurrected Savior said:

> "Old things are done away, and all things have
> become new. Therefore I would that ye should be
> perfect even as I, or your Father who is in heaven
> is perfect" (3 Ne. 12:46-48; cf. D&C 22).

The Restored Kingdom From the Tree of Life Symbol
The 7 seals of the book John saw pertain to the 1000
year periods of the earth's temporal existence after the
Fall (D&C 77:7). Archbishop Ussher gave Adam's date
as 4004 BC and Jesus' birth as 4 BC. Thus, according
to his chronology, if Jesus were born in 1 BC, there
would be no 0 BC, and Adam's date would have been
4001 BC. With this in mind, consider the following:

When John saw the 7 seals opened, he saw 4
symbols—the bow, the sword, the balance, and the altar
(Rev. 6:2, 4, 5, and 9). Four signifies that the message
pertains to the whole earth. Using the 1260-year tree
of life symbol (Diagram 2.4), the bow is the vertical
diameter line of the 1260-year circle (401 years) + the
3:00 p.m. radial line (200 years) + the right half of the
720-year circle (360 years). The sum is 961 years. The
length of the sword equals 802 years (pp. 70, 123, and
Diagram 14.3). The balance is the equilateral triangle
(1203 years) + the bottom half of the 1260-year circle
(630 years). This sum is 1833 years. The altar is the
equilateral triangle (1203 years) + the bottom half of
the 1260-year circle (630 years) + the horizontal
diameter of the 1260-year circle. This sum is 2234
years. The combined sum equals 5830 years. If we add
5830 years to 4001 BC, with no 0 BC, we come to AD
1830, the year the kingdom of God was restored.

Chapter 9

KIRTLAND TEMPLE VISIT

> "We saw the [Son of Man]... His eyes were as a
> flame of fire; the hair of his head was white like
> the pure snow; his countenance shone above the
> brightness of the sun; and his voice was as the
> sound of the rushing of great waters, even the
> voice of Jehovah, saying: I am the first and the
> last [Alpha and Omega]..." (D&C 110:1-4).

Dedication week in the Kirtland Temple was set to coincide with Passion Week, 27 March (the Triumphal Entry in Jerusalem) to 3 April (the Resurrection). It was 16 years after the First Vision. Sixteen years as 4^2 *years* emphasize that the keys *restored* then would enable all kindreds to be gathered from the *four quarters of the earth* and that the *whole earth* would be smitten with a curse unless the hearts of the children *turned* to (were sealed to) the fathers (D&C 110:11-15).

The Kirtland Temple event of 3 April was similar to the Mount of Transfiguration event (Matt. 17:1-3). This similarity suggests that the *restoration* which occurred in the Kirtland Temple should be 6 *years* from the time the Church was organized and the gift of the Holy Ghost made available to newly baptized members. Recall that Jesus had asked Simon Peter: "Whom do men say that I the Son of Man am?" After Peter answered that he knew Jesus was the Christ, the Son of the living God, Jesus said: "Blessed art thou, Simon Bar-jona; for flesh and blood hath not revealed it unto thee, but my Father which is in heaven. And I say also unto thee, That thou art Peter, and upon this rock I will build my church; and the gates of *hell* (6) shall not prevail against it. And I will give unto thee the keys of the kingdom..." (Matt. 16:13-19; cf. D&C 128:10). It was 6 *days* thereafter that Peter, James, and John were taken to the Mount of Transfiguration (Matt. 17:1). Following the pattern used to teach Abraham the age of accountability (p. 3), this suggests that a similar event would occur 6 *years* from AD 6 April 1830, that is, 6 *years* from the time the gift of the Holy Ghost was made available to enable Church members to testify that Jesus is the Christ, and to keep the gates of hell (6) from prevailing against them.

The Kirtland Temple Visit
  From the Chief Cornerstone
The date the Son of Man, Moses, Elias, and Elijah appeared in the Kirtland Temple was set in the 1260-day cornerstone. Joseph Smith was told that if he lived until 1890 *years* from Christ's birth he would see the face of the Son of Man (D&C 130:15). This suggests that a term of 1890 *days* would be associated with Joseph seeing the face of the Son of Man. This 1890-day term is also suggested in a statement Peter made when he came down from the Mount of Transfiguration after seeing Moses and Elijah. He said to the Master: "...it is good for us to be here: if thou wilt, let us make here three tabernacles; one for thee [the Son of Man], and one for Moses, and one for Elias [Elijah]" (Matt. 17:4). This suggests a term equal to three rounds of the center 630-day circle in Diagram 9.1, or 1890 days.

To 1890 days should be added a term representing the spiritual plane. The spiritual plane is symbolized by the downward-pointing equilateral triangle. The sum of the lines forming this triangle is 300 days.

Revelation   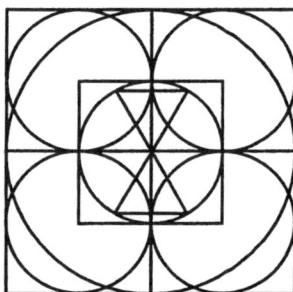   Scripture

Joseph Smith   Priesthood

0, 1260 days

Diagram 9.1

Therefore, we have the following simple equation for the date of the visit of the Son of Man, Moses, Elias, and Elijah in the Kirtland Temple:

$06/04/1830_{\text{Church organized}}$

$+ 1890 \text{ days}_{\text{seeing the Son of Man, Moses, and Elijah}}$

$+ 300 \text{ days}_{\text{spiritual plane}}$

$= 03/04/1836_{\text{Kirtland Temple Visit}}$ (8)

On Sunday, AD 3 April 1836, the Son of Man, Moses, Elias,[1] and Elijah appeared in succession and

---

[1]Joseph Fielding Smith thought this Elias was Noah, but said it was not known (*Answers to Gospel Questions*, 3:139-140; *Church History and Modern Revelation*, 2:49). Apparently, John the Baptist was also present on the Mount of Transfiguration (Matt. 17:9-13).

restored their respective keys (D&C 110:1-4; 11-16). Moses restored the keys to gather Israel; Elias committed the dispensation of the gospel of Abraham; and Elijah restored the sealing powers. The 300 (3 x 10²) days emphasize the importance of faithful completion of temple ordinances and of their being sealed by the Holy Spirit of Promise. The 1890 days (70 x 3³ days) emphasize the promise to faithful Church members that they would become as numerous as the stars of heaven (Gen. 22:15-18). The 3³ days (27 days) references the moon's *sidereal* orbit (p. 9). Written as 14 x 5 x 3³ days, the 1890 *days* also emphasize the punishment to unfaithful Church members—they would fall as stars from heaven if they are unfaithful to the ordinances of the Melchizedek Priesthood. The number 5 pertains to punishments (Smith's Bible Dictionary, "Number").

The Year AD 1890
The year AD 1890 was 70 (14 x 5) years from the First Vision. It ended a 2520-*year* period during which the Lord had *turned away his face* from Israel due to disobedience (Lev. 26:18; HC 5:336). Written as 70 x 6² years, 2520 *years* emphasize *rescue* from Satan's great chain. The 66 were invited to join the 4 (pp. 36-38) to feast on "fat things, of wine on the lees well refined, that the earth would come to know that the mouths of the prophets shall not fail. Yea, a supper of the house of the Lord, well prepared, unto which all nations shall be invited. First, the rich and the learned, the wise and the noble; And after that cometh the day of my power; then shall the poor, the lame, and the blind, and the deaf, come in unto the marriage of the Lamb and partake of the supper of the Lord" (D&C 58:8-11).

Alpha and Omega
The description Joseph Smith gave of the Son of Man in the Kirtland Temple is similar to John's description when he saw him on the Isle of Patmos (Rev. 1:11-18). At both appearances the Son of Man said that he was Alpha and Omega, the first and the last (Rev. 1:8; D&C 110:4; cf. 35:1; 38:1; 95:17). Alpha and Omega signs are seen in the chief cornerstone.

The Alpha signs are formed by two lines of the equilateral triangles in the center circle in Diagram 9.1. Omega signs are formed by the semicircles in the center square together with two horizontal connecting lines from the center of the lines of the inner square to the center of the lines of the outer square. Using *years* as the unit of measure to represent *restoration* and *redemption*, count the lines and semi-circle which make up an Alpha and Omega sign:

$$\Lambda = 100 + 100 = 200 \text{ years; and}$$
$$\Omega = 100 + 315 + 100 = 515 \text{ years.}$$

Alpha and Omega and YHWH
YHWH signs are also seen in the 1260-year cornerstone. YHWH equals 1805 years (p. 49). The total of YHWH + Alpha and Omega in the 1260-year cornerstone equals 2520 years or fulness of time (7 x 360 years). The message is directed to Israel. It pertains to the gospel and the sacred ordinances and covenants of the temple. The 200 years relate to Alpha signifying the mountain (temples) where light and truth are revealed. The 515 years correlate with the temple in Jerusalem (p. 32). The message includes: First, the principles and ordinances of the gospel which were in

the beginning of the earth would be in the end of the earth also (the four 100's, two in ∧ and two in Ω) (cf. Moses 6:7). Second, in the end of the earth the gospel would be in the Book of Mormon, the new covenant (D&C 84:57) (315 in Ω, Diagram 6.3). Third, temple ordinances and covenants revealed in the first dispensation would be restored to Joseph Smith in the last dispensation (the dispensation of the fulness of times) (∧ + Ω + YHWH = 200 + 515 + 1805 = 2520). And fourth, in the end a temple would stand where the Zerubbabel Temple once stood (515 = Ω).

The Judgment of God (Daniel)
The 1260-year cornerstone clearly shows that Joseph Smith is linked to Jesus Christ of the New Testament who is Jehovah of the Old Testament. YHWH + Alpha and Omega equal seven times. Thus, the seven times punishment noted by Moses is God's punishment:

> "If ye will not hearken unto me, and will not do all these commandments,...I will set my face against you, and ye shall be slain before your enemies: they that hate you shall reign over you; and ye shall flee when none pursueth you. And if ye will not yet for all this hearken unto me, then I will punish you seven times more for your sins" (Lev. 26:14, 17-18).

To modern Israel the Lord said:

> "Every man must repent or suffer, for I, God, am endless. Wherefore, I revoke not the judgments which I shall pass, but woes shall go forth... Nevertheless, it is not written that there shall be

no end to this torment, but it is written *endless torment*... I will explain unto you this mystery... I am endless, and the punishment which is given from my hand is endless punishment, for Endless is my name. Wherefore—Eternal punishment is God's punishment. Endless punishment is God's punishment. Wherefore, I command you to repent, and keep the commandments which you have received by the hand of my servant Joseph Smith, Jun., in my name; And it is by my almighty power that you have received them. Therefore, I command you to repent—repent, lest I smite you by the rod of my mouth...and your sufferings be sore—how sore you know not, how exquisite you know not, yea, how hard to bear you know not. For behold, I, God, have suffered these things for all, that they might not suffer if they would repent" (D&C 19:5-16).

God's punishment is endless because Endless is his name, not because it is endless *per se*. God has commanded us to repent and keep the commandments he has given through Joseph Smith (and his successors). The ratio 6/5 symbolizes punishment as a result of becoming subject to Satan. This life is the time to prepare to meet God. Those who disregard covenants made in the temple (symbolized by a mountain or pyramid), and do not repent, become subject to Satan in eternity (circle). (Alma 34:32-36.) This may be symbolized numerically by the equation: π (pi) $= 6/5 \times \phi^2$ (phi²). Pi is the constant (3.1416) of a circle equal to its circumference divided by its diameter; and phi is a constant (1.618) known as the golden section. The Great Pyramid in Egypt was constructed so as to reveal the golden section (p. 30).

Chapter 10

JOSEPH SMITH AND DANIEL'S TIMES

> "The fourth beast shall be the fourth kingdom upon earth, which shall be diverse from all kingdoms, and shall devour the whole earth, and shall tread it down, and break it in pieces.... and they shall be given into his hand until a time, and times and the dividing of a time (Dan. 7:23-25).

Joseph Smith received "the keys of the kingdom, and of the dispensation of the fulness of times" from Peter, James, and John (D&C 128:10, 20). Joseph's ministry should be related to Jesus' 1260-day ministry by the *fulness factor* (7) since he represented Israel, and Israel is compared to God's Firstborn (Ex. 4:22). Following the patterns discussed previously, it can be shown that Joseph Smith's days and years were numbered in sacred writ and set forever in the geometrical symbolism of the chief cornerstone. While in Liberty Jail, the Lord said to Joseph Smith:

> "Hold on thy way, and the priesthood shall remain with thee; for their bounds are set, they cannot pass. Thy days are known, and thy years shall not be numbered less; therefore, fear not what man can do, for God shall be with you forever and ever" (D&C 122:9).

To demonstrate that Joseph Smith's ministry is related to the Savior's ministry via the fulness factor, we begin with the anniversary date of Jesus' birth in the year of the First Vision, namely, Thursday, AD 6 April 1820. We then add 30 *days* to reference Jesus' 30 *years* of preparation (Num. 4:3; Luke 3:23). This brings us to Friday, AD 5 May 1820. The length of Joseph Smith's ministry, counting *inclusively* from that date, should be 1260 days times the *fulness factor* (1260 days x 7 = 8820 days), at which time the temple of his body would be destroyed by evil designing men (cf. John 2:19-21). There are precisely 8820 days from Friday, AD 5 May 1820, to Thursday, AD 27 June 1844, the day of the Prophet's martyrdom (DC 135:1). Joseph was killed at Carthage Jail. "He fell outward into the hands of his murderers, exclaiming, 'O Lord, my God'" (HC 6:618; cf. Matt. 27:46).

Joseph Smith as President of the High Priesthood
The ministry of Joseph Smith was also related to the seven candlestick symbol through the *fulness factor* (7). On Thursday, AD 26 April 1832, the Prophet was confirmed "president of the high priesthood of the church" by the general council of the Church held in "Zion" [Independence, Missouri] (B.H. Roberts, CHC 1:382). The sum of the semicircles representing the seven candlestick symbol (Diagram 2.4) multiplied by the *fulness factor* is 4410 days [(720/2 + 360/2 + 180/2) days x 7 = 4410 days]. Jesus' ministry of 1260 days times the *reconciliation factor* (3.5) also equals 4410 days. If these 4410 days are added to the anniversary date of the crucifixion in the year of the First Vision, namely, AD 1 April 1820, the result is Thursday, AD 26 April 1832, the day the Prophet was confirmed President of the High Priesthood. Seven *years* later, on AD 26 April 1839, the Apostles left the temple lot in Far West to cross the great waters to promulgate the gospel (D&C 118:4-5). Since the world was still suffering from the spiritual famine of which Amos spoke, this seven years is a reminder of the seven years

of famine anciently which brought about the reunion of the 66 with Joseph's 4 to make up the 70. During the 7000th year period of the earth's temporal existence, Judah will be nourished by the gospel and reunited with Ephraim and will flourish upon the mountains of Israel.

Joseph Smith's Total Life Span
The number of days in Jesus' mortal ministry from baptism to crucifixion was 1260 days. If 1260 days are multiplied by the *fulness factor* (7), the result is 8820 days. If 1260 days are multiplied by the *reconciliation factor* (3.5), the result is 4410 days. The sum total of these three periods equals 14,490 days (1260 days + 4410 days + 8820 days = 14,490 days) (Table 1, p. 29).

Taking 30 *days* to reference the preparation *years* prior to the *public* ministry, and adding 33 *days* to reference Jesus' life-span of 33 *years*,[1] plus 360 *days* to correlate with Jesus' body which he sacrificed for us, the total is 423 *days*. Recall that 360 years was used to find Jesus' birth year from the dedication year of the Zerubbabel Temple; and that temple, as modified by Herod, was the temple to which the Jews thought Jesus was referring when he spoke of the destruction of the temple of his body (pp. 31-33). These 423 *days* correlate with the approximate number of *years* between Jesus' birth and the time Moroni deposited the Book of Mormon plates in the Hill Cumorah. This begs the question: "What is the difference between 14,490 days and the 423 days noted above?" The difference is 14,067 days. This begs a follow-up question: "Who

---

[1]Jesus' life span was actually 5 days short of a full 33 years.

lived 14,067 days, received the record from the Hill Cumorah, and was martyred?" He will be the person through whom the Lord would restore his gospel and kingdom, and receive direction to build temples in preparation for the Savior's coming. Counting *inclusively*, there are precisely 14,067 days from Monday, AD 23 December 1805, to Thursday, AD 27 June 1844.

There is no person other than Joseph Smith, Jr., who fits the descriptions given in scripture for the person through whom Jesus Christ would restore his kingdom in the latter-days. Joseph Smith is tied directly to the mortal ministry of Jesus Christ and the message contained in Jesus' 42 generation descent from Abraham as noted by Matthew (JST Matt. 1:1-5). Joseph Smith is the head of the dispensation of the fulness of times. His days were numbered in sacred writ and forever set in the geometrical symbolism of the chief cornerstone (D&C 122:9).

Daniel and Joseph Smith's Martyrdom
Daniel pointed directly to the martyrdom of the Prophet Joseph Smith 1290 days from the time the Nauvoo Charter was signed by the Governor of the State of Illinois on Wednesday, AD 16 December 1840 (Dan. 12:11; HC 4:239-249). The government, both State and Federal, should have upheld the law and thereby prevented the martyrdom of the Prophet. No doubt, the bloodshed experienced by the United States during the Civil War, and particularly the bloodshed which occurred in Illinois and Missouri during that war were in large measure the result of that failure.

Brigham Young came 1335 days[2] following the signing of the Nauvoo Charter and began to transact business under it in place of Joseph Smith. Two days earlier, appropriately on Thursday, AD 8 August 1844, Brigham Young was transfigured before the people and seemed to have the appearance of Joseph Smith (HC 7:231-242). This was taken by the people as a sign that they should follow Brigham Young. The fact that Daniel foresaw these 1335 days (Dan. 12:12) is evidence that Daniel knew how leadership succession would take place in the latter-day kingdom. The authority is in the hands of the Twelve Apostles when the President of the Church passes away, and the senior member of the Twelve is sustained as the President, Prophet, Seer, and Revelator of the Church. This is the pattern the Lord has set.

> "Joseph Smith...has done more, save Jesus only, for the salvation of men in this world, than any other man that ever lived in it. In the short space of twenty years, he has brought forth the Book of Mormon...; has sent the fulness of the everlasting gospel...to the four quarters of the earth; has brought forth revelations and commandments which compose this book of Doctrine and Covenants, and many other wise documents and instructions for the benefit of the children of men; gathered many thousands of the Latter-day Saints, founded a great city, and left a...name that cannot be slain. He lived great, and he died great in the eyes of God and his people..." (D&C 135:3).

---

[2]The 1335 days are Alpha and Omega in the 1260-day tree of life symbol (p. 51).

Chapter 11

WESTERN MIGRATION OF THE SAINTS

> "The Word and Will of the Lord concerning the Camp of Israel in their journeyings to the West: Let all the people of the Church of Jesus Christ of Latter-day Saints, and those who journey with them, be organized into companies, with a covenant and promise to keep all the commandments and statutes of the Lord our God" (D&C 136:1-2).

A parallel for the fleeing of the latter-day saints into the mountains of Western America and the burning of the Nauvoo Temple is the fleeing of the Christians in into the mountains following the threat against Jerusalem by Cestus Gallus in AD 66. This was apparently 1290 *days* before the AD 70 abomination of desolation by Titus (Dan. 12:11; JS-M 1:13) when the temple in Jerusalem was burned and utterly destroyed in the same month and on the same day of the month as was Solomon's temple. Therefore, we might expect the date of the arrival of the saints in the Salt Lake Valley to be found in the squared 1290-*year* circle. Using the 9R pattern, the product ($9R_{1290}$) equals 1847.78 years.

In AD July 1847, the first saints arrived in the mountains of the Salt Lake Valley. The man who led them was the same man (Brigham Young) who came 1335 days (Dan. 12:12) following the signing of the Nauvoo Charter by the Governor of Illinois and began to transact business in place of Joseph Smith.

Jeremiah
The pioneer trek west was seen in vision by Jeremiah. He saw that the Lord turned the sorrow of the saints into joy. He saw them dancing and rejoicing in song:

"For there shall be a day, that the watchmen upon the mount Ephraim shall cry, Arise ye, and let us go up to Zion unto the Lord our God....Sing with gladness for Jacob, and shout among the chief of the nations: publish ye, praise ye, and say, O Lord, save thy people, the remnant of Israel. Behold, I will bring them from the north country, and gather them from the coasts of the earth, and with them the blind and the lame, the woman with child and her that travaileth with child together: a *great company* shall return *thither.*   They shall come with weeping, and with supplications, will I lead them: I will cause them to walk by the rivers of waters in a straight way, wherein they shall not stumble; for I am a father to Israel, and Ephraim is my firstborn. Hear the word of the Lord, O ye nations, and declare it in the isles afar off, and say, He that scattered Israel will gather him, and keep him, as a shepherd doth his flock. For the Lord hath redeemed Jacob, and ransomed him from the hand of him that was stronger than he. Therefore, *they shall come and sing in the height of Zion,* and flow together to the goodness of the Lord, for wheat, and for wine, and for oil, and for the young of the flock and of the herd; and their soul shall be as a watered garden; and they shall not sorrow any more at all. *Then shall the virgin rejoice in the dance, both young men and old together: for I will turn their mourning into joy, and will comfort them, and make them rejoice from their sorrow....*And my people shall be satisfied with my goodness, saith the Lord. (Jer. 31:6-14; emphasis added; see also Is. 26:20-21 relating to the time when the Lord will come out of his place to cleanse the earth.)

Chapter 12

WARS AMONG THE NATIONS

> "The time will come that war will be poured out upon all nations... For behold, the Southern States shall be divided against the Northern States, and the Southern States will call on other nations, even the nation of Great Britain, as it is called, and they shall also call upon other nations, in order to defend themselves against other nations; and then war shall be poured out upon all nations.... Wherefore, stand ye in holy places, and be not moved, until the day of the Lord come; for behold, it cometh quickly" (D&C 87:2-3, 8).

The gospel is the means of saving the house of Israel from the famine of which Amos spoke (Amos 8:11) and of judging the nations (2 Ne. 25:22-23). The Lord promised that all kindreds of the earth would be blessed with the blessings of the gospel through the seed of Abraham (1 Ne. 22:9; Abr. 2:11). This could not happen unless the Lord would make bare his arm in the eyes of all nations; therefore, the Lord God would do so in his due time (1 Ne. 22:10-11; Is. 52:10; Rev. 11:6-13; D&C 1:14; 45:44-48; 88:88-93; 90:9-10).

To date wars have served to open the doors of nations for the preaching of the gospel. World Wars I and II were in partial fulfillment of Joseph Smith's 1832 prophecy on war. War *began* to be poured out upon *all nations* in World War I after Great Britain called upon other nations to defend itself against other nations. World War I began precisely 70 years after the martyrdom of the Prophet Joseph Smith. These 70 *years* reference the eventual *reunification* of Judah and Ephraim. Seventy years from Thursday, AD 27 June 1844, brings us to Sunday, AD 27 June 1914. The next day, on Monday, AD 28 June 1914, Ferdinand and Sophie, duchess of Hohenberg, were assassinated while driving through the streets of Sarejevo. This event triggered World War I. This date was 2520 years from the time Daniel was taken captive into Babylon. Forty-two months (*3.5 years* or 1260 days) after the 1st World War was triggered Jerusalem was *redeemed* for the *political* return of the Jews (Rev. 13:5; cf. p. 105).

Daniel was taken captive in 606 BC. Twenty years later Jerusalem and its temple were destroyed. The temple was reconstructed and dedicated in 516 BC, but it did not contain the ark and the *Shekinah* had departed. Daniel spoke of an abomination of desolation wherein the Jerusalem temple would again be destroyed (JS-M 1:12-13). This occurred in AD 70. By the use of 1290 *days* (Dan. 12:11), Daniel correlated the flight of the Christians in Judea into the mountains prior to this abomination of desolation, and the migration of the saints under Brigham Young to the mountains of Western America (p. 92). By the use of 1335 *days* (Dan. 12:12), Daniel correlated the building of a temple in the top of the mountains in America (Is. 2:2) and the war which freed Jerusalem for the eventual rebuilding of a temple on the sacred site in Jerusalem. The 9R of the 1335-*year* circle brings us to AD 1912, twenty years *after* the capstone was placed on the Salt Lake Temple. Shortly thereafter, political conditions deteriorated rapidly and World War I began, resulting in Jerusalem being freed for the return of the Jews and the eventual taking of the gospel to them so that there would be no more two nations, but one nation upon the mountains of Israel (Ez. 37:21-22).

President Wilford Woodruff

President Wilford Woodruff foresaw the beginning of wars among the nations of the Gentiles. In remarks given on Sunday, AD 24 June 1894, he said that the destroying angels were sent forth at the time of the dedication of the Salt Lake Temple (AD 6 April 1893), and that they began from that very *day* (AD 24 June 1894) to pour out judgments. He said further that 20 *years* from that time great changes would therefore take place among the nations. These angels were the angels referred to in the Parable of the Wheat and the Tares (Matt. 13:24-30) who, as early as AD 2 January 1831, were ready to reap down the earth (D&C 38:12).[1] "But the Lord said unto them: Pluck not up the tares while the blade is yet tender...lest you destroy the wheat also. Therefore, let the wheat and the tares grow together until the harvest is fully ripe; then ye shall first gather out the wheat from among the tares, and after the gathering of the wheat, behold and lo, the tares are bound in bundles, and the field remaineth to be burned" (DC 86:5-7). These angels may be the four angels which John saw standing on the four corners of the earth (Rev. 7:1). They may be four translated beings, John and the three Nephites (3 Ne. 28:6, 30; LeGrand Richards, *Israel! Do You Know?* [Deseret Book Co., 6th Printing, 1967], pp. 230-233).

The Return of the Jews to Palestine

Palestine was freed for the political return of the Jews precisely 1260 days (42 30-day months) from the time

---

[1]*Young Woman's Journal,* Vol. 5, pp. 512-513.

World War I began in accordance with John's prophecy (Rev. 13:5). One of the seven heads of the *image* (HC 5:345; see also 5:341) which John saw rise up out of the *sea* (Rev. 13:1; 17:15) was wounded to death, but it was healed, and all the world wondered after the image, and it had power to continue 42 months (Rev. 13:3, 5). But as John said, "He that leadeth into captivity shall go into captivity; and he that killeth with the sword must be killed with the sword" (Rev. 13:10).

If 1260 days are added to Monday, AD 28 June 1914, the day World War I was initiated, the result is Monday, AD 9 December 1917. On Monday, AD 9 December 1917, a force made up of troops from Great Britain, which is *north and west* of Palestine, and from New Zealand, part of *the land of sinim* (Is. 49:12), reached and secured Jerusalem. Two days later, on Wednesday, AD 11 December 1917, the chief of the British Expeditionary Force for the whole Near East, Sir Edmund Allenby, arrived at Jerusalem to take command of the Holy City. As an expression of reverence for the city, General Allenby dismounted his horse and walked on foot through Jaffa Gate.[2]

On AD 6 April 1917, the United States officially entered World War I, just eight months before Jerusalem was freed from Turkish control. Though Palestine was freed for the political return of the Jews in the year AD 1917, the Jews did not have political control of Jerusalem until the Jubilee Year fifty years later (AD 1967). This was 2520 360-day years from the dedication

[2]Encyclopedia Britannica, "World War I".

of the Zerubbabel Temple in 516 BC, suggesting that a temple would again grace the sacred spot.

Joseph Smith prophesied that the wars leading up to the Second Coming would begin in South Carolina (D&C 87:1-2, 6-8). Civil War in the United States began on AD 12 April 1861. The Southern States called upon Great Britain to help defend themselves from the Northern States as prophesied. The Prophet said further that war would be poured out upon all nations when Great Britain called upon other nations to defend itself against other nations (DC 87:3; cf. 1 Ne. 14:16). This occurred beginning in World War I.

World War II and Beyond
John saw a seven-headed image rise up "out of the sea," wicked political powers arising out of the ancient Roman Empire (Rev. 13:1; cf. 17:15). One of its heads was wounded to death, but its deadly wound was healed (Rev. 13:3). He saw another image arise, which exercised all the power of the first (Rev. 13:11-12). If these degenerate kingdoms also include those which caused World Wars I and II, then the archetypical man John referred to by 666 (Rev. 13:18) might be identified in the 1260-year cornerstone. World War II lasted exactly *6 years*, from 1 September 1939, when Nazi Germany invaded Poland, to 1 September 1945, when Japan signed surrender papers aboard the *Missouri*. (The Nephite nation was destroyed in a *60-year* war.)

The 666 seems to relate to the great chain by which Satan leads degenerate kingdoms in the latter days. Anciently, the 66 souls in Jacob's household went into Egypt, where, with Joseph's 4, they became the 70 and were saved from the famine (Gen. 46:26-27). By the latter-day the 70 were divided, scattered and dispersed among all nations. The gathering began with Joseph's seed, represented by the 4. They gathered to the land of Zion, and the 66 were among the nations where the great and abominable church held power (cf. 1 Ne. 13:4-6; 14:10). They were invited to join Joseph. Israel was warned to flee, Joseph to Zion and Judah to Jerusalem, but not to flee in haste, but rather to prepare all things (D&C 133:12-15; cf. 58:9); otherwise, they would suffer from famine, and from the hand of a man identified by the number 666 in the 1260-year cornerstone, and eventually from the three woes (Rev. 9 & 11) to which 666 may ultimately refer. The man identified in the 1260-year cornerstone by 666 is a *type* personifying wicked leaders in the last days whom Satan leads by his great chain (Moses 7:26; Alma 12:11).

666 = DCLXVI

The number 666 in Roman Numerals is DCLXVI. Using the center square of the 1260-year cornerstone (Diagram 12.1), "count the number of the beast: for it is the number of a man" (Rev. 13:18) who would rise to power "x" number of years from the birth of Jesus Christ. It would be seven times or 2520 years from the time Jerusalem was destroyed (587-586 BC) and also an hour of judgment (42 years) away from the time Joseph Smith would have been 85 years old (HC 5:336).

Step one is to count the number of years in the D of DCLXVI. Look at the vertical center line in the inner square of Diagram 12.1 and the right-hand semicircle. This forms the D. C is the left-hand semicircle, and so forth:

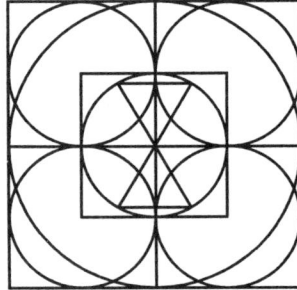

0, 1260 years

Diagram 12.1

D = 200.5 + 315 = 515.5 years;
C = 315 years;
L = 200.5 + 100.25 = 300.75 years;
X = 4 x 100.25 = 401 years;
V = 200.5 years.; and finally,
I = 200.5 years.

Symbolically, the individual terms of DCLXVI represent things which would *rescue* the nations from the woes which will come in the last days as a result of their being held captive by Satan's great chain. These things are the First Vision and Melchizedek Priesthood; the Book of Mormon and Bible; the first principles and ordinances of the gospel; temples; the everlasting covenants and sword of truth; and spiritual enlightenment. The sum of the individual terms in DCLXVI = 1933.25 years.

In AD March 1933 Adolf Hitler came to power.[3] Hitler is archetypical of wicked leaders in the last days who would seek so-called *ethnic cleansing* and carry out genocide. The power which enabled Hitler, Stalin and others to destroy the innocent fits the pattern described in scripture (Rev. 13; 1 Ne. 14:16-17; D&C 45:26; 87:3). If those of Judah had fled to Jerusalem (D&C 133:13) after it was first freed for their return at the end of World War I, they would have been spared the holocaust. This was an awful warning regarding a future abomination of desolation after which the Lord will set foot on the Mount of Olives (JS-M 1:32; D&C 133:20).

The year AD 1933 is 2520 years from the time of the destruction of Jerusalem in 587-586 BC. An hour of judgment preceded AD 1933 according to Joseph Smith (HC 5:336). Regarding this hour Joseph Smith said the following:

> "I was once praying earnestly upon this subject, and a voice said unto me, 'My son, if thou livest until thou art eighty-five years of age, thou shalt see the face of the Son of Man.' I was left to draw my own conclusions concerning this; and I took the liberty to conclude that if I did live to that time, He would make his appearance or I shall go where He is. I prophesy in the name of the Lord God, and let it be written—the Son of Man will not come in the clouds of heaven till I am eighty-five years old. Then read the 14th chapter of Revelation, 6th and 7th verses—'And I saw another angel fly in the midst of heaven, having the everlasting gospel to preach unto them

---

[3]Encyclopedia Britannica, "Hitler".

that dwell on the earth, and to every nation, and kindred, and tongue, and people, saying, with a loud voice, Fear God and give glory to Him, for the hour of His judgment is come.' And Hosea, 6th chapter, After two days, etc.,—2520 years; which brings it to 1890. The coming of the Son of Man never will be—never can be till the judgments spoken of for this hour are poured out: which judgments are commenced. Paul says, 'Ye are the children of light, and not of darkness, that that day should overtake you as a thief in the night.' It is not the design of the Almighty to come upon the earth and crush it and grind it to powder, but he will reveal it to His servants the prophets" (HC 5:336-337).

The year AD 1890 is 70 years from the First Vision of Joseph Smith. An hour of the Lord's time is about 42 years of man's time. The hour referred to by Joseph Smith began sometime between AD 23 December 1890 and AD 22 December 1891. If 42 years is added to AD 1891, the result is AD 1933.

Joseph Smith also said that the year AD 1890 ended a 2520-year period. Twenty-five hundred and twenty 360-day years earlier Lehi and his family were settled in Bountiful and preparing to go to the promised land. On AD 6 April 1893 the Salt Lake Temple was dedicated. This was 2520 360-day years from the time Lehi and his family entered the ship and set sail for the promised land (2 Ne. 18:8). Lehi was one of the prophets who had warned the Jews that if they did not repent Jerusalem would be destroyed. They sought his life so he and his family departed the land of Jerusalem in 600 BC. (1 Ne. 1:4, 13, 18-20; 2:1-4; 18:8.)

A Warning to Modern Israel
The Lord did not say that all individuals would be spared the difficulties caused by the wickedness of the last days. He said that a desolating scourge would go forth from time to time, but Zion as a whole would escape if she observed to do all things whatsoever the Lord commanded her (D&C 5:19; 97:25; Moses 7:61).

And so the admonition continues to go forth: "Go ye out from among the nations, even from Babylon, from the midst of wickedness, which is spiritual Babylon. But...let not your flight be in haste, but let all things be prepared before you; and he that goeth, let him not look back lest sudden destruction shall come upon him" (D&C 133:14-15). Spiritual Babylon is the world which shall end (JS-M 1:31).

Opening the Doors of the Nations
The Son of Man set his face against Israel because of disobedience (Lev. 26:17). In AD 1890 he began to turn his face back toward Israel. John the Revelator described the face of the Son of Man. He said that his eyes were as a flame of fire, that his voice was as the sound of many waters, and that out of his mouth went a sharp two-edged sword (Rev. 1:14-16). Nephi said that the justice of God is as the brightness of a flaming fire (1 Ne. 15:30). Many waters are as multitudes, and nations, and tongues (Rev. 17:15). A sharp two-edged sword is the sword of the Spirit which is the word of God or the gospel (Eph. 6:17; JST John 1:1).

Considering that the gospel was restored among the Gentiles through Joseph Smith, it seems that AD 1890 began a transition period during which the Lord would begin to open the way for the gospel to be taken to the natural remnants of the house of Israel. In AD 1893 the temple which Isaiah saw in the top of the mountains was dedicated (Is. 2:2). A little more than 20 years thereafter, World War I broke out.

World Wars I and II served to open the doors of the nations for the preaching of the gospel. Unfortunately, it appears that the Gentiles, in general, will not receive the gospel, "for they perceive not the light" (D&C 45:29). Therefore, wars will continue to be poured out from time to time until Christ comes and the consumption decreed makes a full end of all nations (DC 87:6). Those who fight against Zion shall fall into the pit which they digged to ensnare the covenant people of the Lord (1 Ne. 22:14). Although the Jews have returned politically to Jerusalem, they remain generally in unbelief, and will apparently remain so until the times of the Gentiles are fulfilled and the Lord comes to them (Rom. 11:25; D&C 45:25).

Sometime in the beginning of the 7000 year period of the earth's temporal existence, the gospel will go preferentially to the Jews, and their reunification with Ephraim will be *completed* as implied by 7000 written as 70×10^2. "The arm of the Lord shall be revealed in power in convincing the nations, the heathen nations, the house of Joseph, of the gospel of their salvation" (D&C 90:9-10). After the warning voice has gone forth for the last time and the saints have been gathered from the four quarters of the earth, there will be another abomination of desolation (JS-M 1:27, 31-32). To save the Jews from utter destruction, the Messiah will come to them. For 1260 days prior to that time, two prophets will preach the gospel in Jerusalem (Rev. 11:3). They shall have power to shut the heavens, that it rains not in the days of their prophecy, and to turn waters to blood, and to smite the earth with plagues, as often as they will (Rev. 11:6; 1 Ne. 22:11). During this 42 months, Jerusalem shall be trodden down by the Gentiles (Rev. 11:2). After these *3.5 years*, the Savior will set his foot upon the Mount of Olives (Rev. 11:13; D&C 45:48; 88:89) and *redeem* Jerusalem for the *spiritual* return of the Jews (Is. 52:9-10; p. 95). In the words of Parley P. Pratt, "the Messiah comes, convulses the earth, overthrows the army of the Gentiles, delivers the Jews, cleanses Jerusalem, cuts off all wickedness from the earth, raises the saints from the dead, brings them with him, and commences his reign of a thousand years" (*Voice of Warning*, p. 34; cf. Rev. 20:6; 1 Ne. 22:20-21; D&C 43:30; 45:44-48; 88:95-98).

YHWH + Alpha and Omega + 666

YHWH + Alpha and Omega = 2520 years or *seven times* in the 1260-year cornerstone (pp. 48-49, 84-85). If the 1933 years associated with 666 is added to 2520 years, the result is 4453 years. Counting 4453 years back from the end of the 6th day (AD 2000),[4] we have 2453 BC, the birth year of Shem (2453 BC).[5] From

---

[4]The year AD 2000 is approximately 4410 360-day years from the Flood of Noah (see Table 1.1). The number 4410 is 3.5 (the reconciliation factor) times the 1260-year cornerstone.

[5]Archbishop Ussher gave the date for Adam as 4004 BC and the date of Jesus' birth as 4 BC instead of 1 BC. Therefore, if the date for Adam was 4001 BC, then the date for Shem would be 2453 BC.

this symbolism it appears that he was Melchizedek after whom the Holy Priesthood after the order of the Son of God was named (D&C 107:2-3).

The message of YHWH + Alpha and Omega + 666 seems to be that those who unite with Israel through the restored Priesthood and keep the commandments given through Joseph Smith will be preserved when the *woes* described in Revelation 9 and 11 come upon the earth. In a broad sense, 666 seems to refer to the woes which will come upon those who are held captive by Satan's great chain. There will be three woes, in essence, one for each 6 in 666. "And wo unto all those who come not unto this priesthood which ye have received" (D&C 84:42).

All those who receive the Aaronic and Melchizedek Priesthoods, and magnify their calling, shall be sanctified by the Spirit unto the renewing of their bodies. According to the promise, they will receive all that the Father has. (D&C 84:33-40.)

Enoch, Zion, and the Melchizedek Priesthood
Following the exodus the children of Israel were offered the Melchizedek Priesthood. But they hardened their hearts and therefore could not endure God's presence; thus, God took Moses and the Holy Priesthood out of their midst, and the Lesser Priesthood and preparatory gospel continued among them.

There were 430 years from the time Terah died and Abraham left Haran and received the promises of the Holy Priesthood (Abr. 2:11), and the *exodus* and the *birth* of the nation of Israel under the law of Moses (Gal. 3:17). These 430 years are a reminder to Israel of Enoch's life from birth to translation (Moses 8:1). Enoch was the *7th Patriarch* (Moses 6:12-21). His name means *dedicated*. He was dedicated to the birth of Zion. These 430 years are seen in Diagrams 5.1 and 5.2 with years as the unit of measure. The sum of $9R_{180}$ years plus two 86-year lines equals 430 years. Nine references *birth* and 180 references the *fulness* of Jesus' ministry from baptism to crucifixion, since it lasted 180 *weeks* (7-day periods). The 86-unit lines are the vision lines (see Diagram 5.1, p. 46). The 430 years are thus also a reminder that "where there is no vision, the people perish" (Prov. 29:18), for "without the ordinances and authority of the [Melchizedek Priesthood], the power of godliness is not manifest unto men in the flesh; for without this no man can see the face of God, even the Father, and live" (D&C 84:21-27).

Salvation does not come by the law of Moses, but by the Atonement of Christ. The law was given as a schoolmaster to bring the children of Israel unto Christ, so that the blessings of Abraham (made possible by the Atonement of Christ) might come to all mankind. All mankind may become the children of Christ and receive the *Spirit* through faith in the Lord Jesus Christ, repentance, baptism by immersion for the remission of sins, and the laying on of hands for the gift of the Holy Ghost (Gal. 3:14, 24-27; Mosiah 5:7; A of F 1:4).

Enoch built Zion over 365 *years* (Moses 7:68). Thus, each of the 365 and ¼ *days* of each earth *year* is a reminder to people in all the world to seek to bring forth and establish Zion (D&C 6:6), and to *dedicate* themselves *fully* to God. To God and the Lamb be glory, honor, and dominion forevermore (D&C 76:119).

Chapter 13

SUB-CORNERSTONES OF THE LATTER-DAY KINGDOM

> "I am...the stone of Israel. He that buildeth upon this rock shall never fall" (D&C 50:43-44).

A *stone* (or rock) is a metaphor for Jesus Christ. He is the *sure foundation* and *Chief Cornerstone* upon which the Church is founded (Is. 28:16; Eph. 2:20; Hel 5:12).

The word *stone* is also a metaphor for hard-hearted gentiles who worship gods made of stone (Deut. 4:27-28). When Jesus saw certain Pharisees and Sadducees come to his baptism, he admonished them to bring forth fruit meet for repentance; and to think not, "We have Abraham [as our father]; for I say unto you, that God is able of these stones to raise up children unto Abraham" through adoption (Matt. 3:7-9; BD "Adoption," p. 604).

Jesus' triumphal entry into Jerusalem on Sunday, AD 27 March 33, 1803 years[1] prior to the first Kirtland Temple dedication session, was greeted with: "Hosanna to the Son of David... Hosanna in the highest" (Matt. 21:9). And some Pharisees said: "Master, rebuke thy disciples." Jesus answered, saying: "I tell you that, if these should hold their peace, the stones would immediately cry out" (Luke 19:35-40), signifying that the earth would quake and the rocks would rend and many saints would come forth from their graves rejoicing and shouting "Hosanna in the highest" (Matt. 27:51-53).

---

[1]This is a *saros* period x 10^2. A *saros* period is 18.03 years. It is a period over which eclipses in the earth-moon system repeat themselves.

Jesus Christ

Jesus said: "Did ye never read the scriptures, The stone which the builders rejected, the same is become the head of the corner..." (JST Matt. 21:44; cf. Ps. 118:22; Zech. 10:4). Jesus Christ became the head of the corner by virtue of his Atonement and Resurrection which enable the unconditional resurrection of all mankind and eternal life on conditions of repentance (the gospel *merism*). Within the Chief Cornerstone are four first level sub-cornerstones (Diagram 2.2): Joseph Smith, Revelation (First Vision), Scripture (Book of Mormon), and the Priesthood (Apostles and Prophets).[2]

Joseph Smith

Under Jesus Christ, Joseph Smith represents the first sub-cornerstone of the restored kingdom. He is the rod which came out of the Stem of Jesse (Is. 11:1; D&C 113:3-4).

The Revelation (First Vision)

The second sub-cornerstone of the restored kingdom is Revelation (First Vision). The Father is the author of the plan of salvation.[3] He has revealed it in the latter-day as promised by the Resurrected Savior to the Nephites (3 Ne. 21:2-4). Joseph Smith related the following experience:

---

[2]Gordon B. Hinckley, Ensign, Nov. 1984, pp. 50-52.

[3]Alma 34:9; 42:5; James E. Talmage, *Jesus the Christ,* 15th Ed., notes, pp. 15-16.

> "I saw a pillar of light exactly over my head, above the brightness of the sun, which descended gradually until it fell upon me.... When the light rested upon me I saw two Personages, whose brightness and glory defy all description, standing above me in the air. One of them spake unto me, calling me by name and said, pointing to the other--This is My Beloved Son. Hear Him" (JS-H 1:17)!

This specific affirmation and commandment of the Father given to Joseph Smith has apparently been made every time that man has seen the Father (JST John 1:19). "Unto Adam, Enoch, Noah, Abraham and Moses the Father revealed himself, attesting the Godship of the Christ, and the fact that the Son was the chosen Savior of mankind."[4] Man is to live by every word which has proceeded forth from the mouth of the Father (DC 84:44; Deut. 8:3; Matt. 4:4).

Jesus took Peter, James and John upon a mountain and they had the following experience:

> "...a bright cloud overshadowed them; and...a voice out of the cloud...said, This is my beloved Son, in whom I am well pleased; hear ye him" (JST Matt. 17:4).

This occurred six *days*[5] after Jesus asked Peter: "Whom do men say that I the Son of Man am?" After Peter answered, saying that he knew Jesus was the

---

[4]James E. Talmage, *Jesus the Christ*, 15th ed. p. 39.

[5]The latter-day parallel suggests that *six years* after the Church is organized the Son of Man, Moses and Elijah would appear.

Christ, the Son of the living God, Jesus said: "Blessed art thou, Simon Bar-jona; for flesh and blood hath not revealed it unto thee, but my Father which is in heaven. And I say also unto thee, That thou art Peter, and upon this rock I will build my church; and the gates of hell shall not prevail against it. And I will give unto thee the keys of the kingdom..." (Matt. 16:13-19).

The Scriptures (Book of Mormon)

The third sub-cornerstone of the restored kingdom is Scripture (Book of Mormon). The Book of Mormon contains the fulness of the everlasting gospel which was taught by the Resurrected Savior to the Nephites (DC 27:5). Through Joseph Smith, the Lord said:

> "Build upon my rock, which is my gospel... (DC 11:24).
>
> If you build up my church, upon the foundation of my gospel and my rock, the gates of hell shall not prevail against you (DC 18:5).

The Book of Mormon is the keystone of our religion.[6]

The Priesthood (Apostles and Prophets)

The fourth sub-cornerstone of the restored kingdom is the Priesthood, the keys and authority of which are held by the First Presidency and the Apostles. The following revelation of the Lord was directed to Oliver Cowdery and David Whitmer:

---

[6]Ezra Taft Benson, Ensign, Nov. 1986, p. 10.

"...I speak unto you, even as unto Paul mine apostle, for you are called even with that same calling with which he was called..." (DC 18:9).

Paul explained to the Ephesians:

"Now therefore ye are no more strangers and foreigners, but fellowcitizens with the saints, and of the household of God. And are built upon the foundation of the apostles and prophets, Jesus Christ himself being the chief corner stone; in whom all the building fitly framed together groweth unto an holy temple in the Lord..." (Eph. 2:18-21).

Much of the gospel symbolism contained in the book of Revelation comes from the seven candlestick and tree of life symbols. It is either a part of these symbols or a different view of it as seen when the flaming sword turns every way to keep the way of the tree of life (Moses 4:31).

The Second Coming of the Son of Man
The Son of Man will come upon the earth in judgment in his own due time and redeem his people and they shall reign with him. For the great millennium shall come of which the prophets have spoken (D&C 43:29-30). Presumably, Thursday, AD 6 April 2000, is 2000 years from the birth of Jesus Christ on Thursday, 6 April 1 BC, but it is not said that the Son of Man will come at that time. No one knows the day or the hour of the Lord's coming, only the Father (Matt 24:36). It is said, however, that he will come sometime in the beginning of the 7th thousand years of the earth's

temporal existence (D&C 77:6, 12). This does not mean that the time is arbitrary. To the contrary, as Elder Bruce R. McConkie has said: "The time is fixed, the hour set...the appointed day can be neither advanced nor delayed. It will come at the decreed moment, chosen before the foundation of the earth was laid, and it can be neither hastened by righteousness nor put off by wickedness. It will be with our Lord's return as it was with his birth to Mary; the time of each coming was fixed by the Father."[7]

No subject is more exciting and motivating to righteous saints than the second coming of the Son of Man in the clouds of heaven, with power and great glory.[8] The coming of the city of Enoch, which was separated from the earth and reserved until the millennial day of righteousness, will be associated with this long awaited event; for the Lord shall bring with him the holy angels and restore all parts of the earth which have heretofore been taken away in the various convulsions which the earth has experienced.[9]

All saints look forward to the day the Lord described to Enoch:

---

[7]Bruce R. McConkie, *A New Witness for the Articles of Faith*, p. 591; cf. D&C 84:119.

[8]Is. 40:5; JS-M 1:26, 36; D&C 45:44.

[9]JST Gen. 9:21-23; 1 Thess. 4:14; Heb. 12:22-24; D&C 45:12; 65:5-6; Moses 7:64; Joseph Young, *History of the Organization of the Seventies* [Salt Lake City: Deseret News, 1878], p. 11; Wandle Mace, "Sayings of Joseph Smith", JSP; MS 1:258; LDS Hymn #48, 4th Verse.

As I live, even so will I come in the last days, in the days of wickedness and vengeance, to fulfil the oath which I have made unto you concerning the children of Noah; And the day shall come that the earth shall rest, but before that day the heavens shall be darkened, and a veil of darkness shall cover the earth; and the heavens shall shake, and also the earth; and great tribulation shall be among the children of men, but my people will I preserve; And righteousness will I send down out of heaven; and truth will I send forth out of the earth, to bear testimony of mine Only Begotten; his resurrection from the dead; yea, and also the resurrection of all men; and righteousness and truth will I cause to sweep the earth as with a flood, to gather out mine elect from the four quarters of the earth, unto a place which I shall prepare, an Holy City, that my people may gird up their loins, and be looking forth for the time of my coming; for there shall be my tabernacle, and it shall be called Zion, a New Jerusalem.... Then shalt thou and all thy city meet them there, and we will receive them into our bosom, and they shall see us; and we will fall upon their necks, and they shall fall upon our necks, and we will kiss each other; and there shall be mine abode, and it shall be Zion, which shall come forth out of all the creations which I have made; and for the space of a thousand years the earth shall rest. (Moses 7:60-64.)

Chapter 14

HE THAT IS WITHOUT SIN

"He that is without sin among you, let him first
cast a stone at her" (John 8:7).

An event which occurred in the temple at Jerusalem
during the feast of Tabernacles provides marvelous
insight into the teaching style, compassion and mission
of Jesus the Christ. The Jewish feast of Tabernacles
was celebrated for 7 days on the 15th to the 21st days
of the 7th ecclesiastical month called Tisri (September-
October). To the 7 days was added an 8th day—"the
last day, that great day of the feast" (John 7:37). The
events of this feast celebrated the sojourning of Moses
and the children of Israel in the wilderness and the
ingathering of the fruits of the year (Feasts, BD p. 673).

The feast of ingathering is symbolic of the
harvest of souls. The Mount of Olives is the place
where Jesus prayed three times[1] and sweat great drops
of blood to enable the harvest of souls. This occurred
"about a stone's cast" away from where the Apostles
waited and slept (Luke 22:41, 44; Matt. 26:36-46).
Being a "stone's cast" away ties the Atonement to Jesus'
response to the scribes and Pharisees regarding the
woman taken in adultery: "He that is without sin
among you, let him first cast a stone at her" (John 8:7).

---

[1]Jesus prayed three times, saying: "O my Father, if it be possible, let this cup pass from me; nevertheless not as I will, but as thou
wilt" (Matt. 26:39, 42, 44). By virtue of his Atonement, Jesus Christ
became our advocate with the Father (D&C 45:3). He stands at the
door and knocks (Rev. 3:20; cf. 2 Ne. 9:41). If he knocks for us, it
shall be opened unto us (Matt. 7:7).

The disciples had urged Jesus to go up to the feast that the people might see the works which he did. There was a sense of pride expressed by his brethren. But Jesus did not yield to this persuasion. John records that after his brethren had gone up to Jerusalem, Jesus also went up, not openly as they had urged, but in secret. (John 7:1-10.)

Teaching in the Temple
On the evening of the 8th day of the feast, Jesus went to the Mount of Olives (John 8:1). Early the next morning, Jesus came into the temple, and people came to him; and he sat down, and taught them (John 8:2).

While Jesus was teaching, certain scribes and Pharisees came to him seeking something of which to accuse him (John 8:6). The scribes were lawyers who developed and applied the law of Moses to the circumstances of the time. They were usually given the title Rabbi meaning *my teacher*. They taught the people but not on their own authority as did Jesus (Matt. 7:29). Their purpose was to reproduce accurately the words of the wise. Because the Lord disregarded the "traditions of the elders" (JST Mark 7:6), they generally opposed him. (Scribes, BD p. 770.)

The Pharisees prided themselves on their strict observance of the law, and on the care with which they avoided contact with things of the Gentiles. Their tendency was to reduce religion to ceremonial rules. They were a major obstacle to the reception of Jesus Christ and his gospel. (Pharisees, BD p. 750.)

A Woman Taken in Adultery

The scribes and Pharisees brought to Jesus a woman taken in adultery. In a sense this woman also represented the Jewish nation who had apostatized from the ways of the Lord (Adultery, BD p. 604). The scribes and Pharisees posed the following question: "Master, this woman was taken in adultery, in the very act. Now Moses in the law commanded us, that such should be stoned; but what sayest thou" (John 8:4-5)? Under the law of Moses adultery was punishable by death (Lev. 20:10), and stoning was the ordinary means of carrying out the penalty (Ex. 17:4). It was required that the witnesses be first to cast a stone and afterwards all the people (Deut. 13:9-10; 17:6-7).

Upon hearing this question, "Jesus stooped down, and with his finger wrote on the ground, as though he heard them not" (John 8:6). Apparently, at this time the death penalty for adultery was no longer used (cf. John 7:19-20). Presumably, the people did not want it, and Roman law did not prescribe it. And in any case it would require the approval of the Roman authorities. In setting the woman in the midst of the people and asking Jesus this question, the scribes and Pharisees had presumably set up a situation which they felt would trap Jesus into answering one way or the other, and therefore they would have something of which to accuse him. If Jesus agreed to stoning, he would be seen as going against the Romans. If he did not agree, he would be seen as going against Moses.

Jesus did not answer as expected. Rather, he stooped down, signifying his condescension, and with his finger wrote on the ground. Though it appeared to the people that he did not hear the question, was he not answering in quiet dignity that his finger wrote the law on tablets of clay and that he had now come to fulfill it and to teach his gospel and establish his kingdom? And if so, might he not have drawn a cruciform to reference diagrammatically the first principles and ordinances of the gospel and that he would willingly submit to be "lifted up" on the Roman cross to save repentant sinners (Diagram 14.1)?

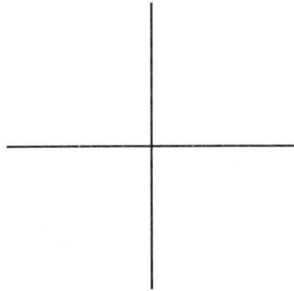

Diagram 14.1

The word of God comes down like the river in the garden of Eden story and divides into the first principles and ordinances of the gospel represented by the lines of the cruciform. Since it appeared to the people that Jesus had not heard the question, his silent response gave the scribes and Pharisees an opportunity to reconsider what they were doing and to cease tempting the Lord their God before they were embarrassed publicly—a privilege they were not giving the woman.

Jesus Lifted Up Himself

Rather than taking advantage of the opportunity to humble themselves before the Lord, the scribes and Pharisees persisted in their attempt to trap Jesus. So when they continued asking Jesus, "he lifted up himself, and said unto them, He that is without sin among you, let him first cast a stone at her" (John 8:7). "Lifting up himself" signifies that no man could take Jesus' life. He would of himself submit to be "lifted up" on the Roman cross to save repentant sinners. That this was John's understanding is evidenced by the change Joseph Smith made to the King James Version of John 8:10 as will be discussed below.

It is generally assumed that Jesus' response means that people should not cast (throw) stones in judgment if they have sins. But if that were the meaning, then Jesus would have been saying that no judgments should be made by mortal man, since no one is without sin. On the other hand, perhaps Jesus' response was intended to show a comparison between the law of Moses and the gospel of Jesus Christ. Jesus often made such comparisons (i.e., Matt. 5:21-22). The law of Moses required that the witnesses to a capital offense be the first to cast a stone and then all the people (Deut. 13:9-10; 17:6-7), but Jesus said unto them, "He that is without sin among you, let him first cast a stone at her." Jesus was the one among them who was without sin, and he was apparently teaching them that before condemning the woman, the stone that the builders were rejecting (JST Matt. 21:44) should first be cast (directed)[2] at the woman to begin the repentance process in an effort to redeem her. Jesus came not to condemn, but to redeem (John 3:17). The whole have no need of a physician, but they that are sick (Mark 2:17). Therefore, "judge not according to your traditions, but judge righteous judgment" (JST John 7:24).

Jesus would come again in a day of judgment; then those who had knowingly and willfully sinned and would not repent in the days of their probation would be condemned, but not by Jesus, rather by their own thoughts and actions (cf. Alma 12:14).

Jesus Raised Up Himself
After giving this verbal response, Jesus again stooped down, and wrote on the ground. In this instance it appears that Jesus was signifying that he would submit to the will of the Father in atoning for the sins of the world. Assuming Jesus drew a cruciform when he first stooped down, perhaps this time he drew a squared circle around the cruciform (Diagram 14.2) to show diagrammatically that the stone which the builders were rejecting would become head of the corner by virtue of the Atonement and Resurrection (Ps. 118:21-22; JST Matt. 21:44). Later, to impress this understanding on the minds of the Apostles, Jesus was "about a stone's cast" away from them when he suffered in the garden

---

[2]See the word "cast" in Webster's Third New International Dictionary, unabridged, 1966: 1b(1):DIRECT; (2) to project or to put forth in a particular direction; (4) to cause to enter or begin a state of activity.

of Gethsemane. The effect of Jesus' drawing the square and the circle around the cruciform would have been to convey a message diagrammatically that if they would believe in him, repent, and be baptized, they would know the truth from the Comforter, and the truth would free them from Satan's great chain. They would then have the light of life in this world and eternal life in eternity.

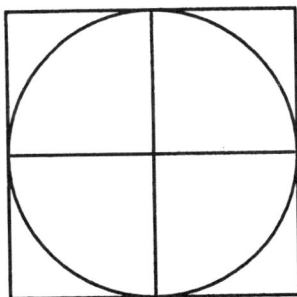

Diagram 14.2

The scribes and Pharisees who heard Jesus verbal response and saw what he wrote, "being convicted by their own conscience, went out one by one, beginning at the eldest, even unto the last; and Jesus was left alone, and the woman standing in the midst of the temple. When Jesus had raised up himself, and saw none of her accusers, and the woman standing, he said unto her, Woman, where are those thine accusers? hath no man condemned thee" (JST John 8:9-10; cf. 2:19)? The King James Version says, "When Jesus had lifted up himself", as if he were simply standing up. But Joseph Smith changed this to read "raised up himself", signifying that Jesus was communicating symbolically that he had the power to resurrect himself and all mankind, unconditionally. Joseph Smith did not change "lifted up himself" in the first instance noted in John 8:7, meaning that in the first instance Jesus was communicating symbolically that he would voluntarily submit to the Roman cross to save repentant sinners.

The Happy Result

The Joseph Smith Translation of this marvelous account clarifies the outcome as regards the woman. In response to the Lord's inquiry, "Where are those thine accusers? hath no man condemned thee", she answered, "No man, Lord." And Jesus said, "Neither do I condemn thee [signifying that he was not the Son of a mortal man, but rather the Son of God (cf. John 8:13-19)]; go, and sin no more. And the woman glorified God from that hour, and believed on his name" (JST John 8:11). The happy result would be the harvest of a soul, commemorated forever by this feast of Tabernacles. The woman glorified God and believed on his name, suggesting that her *repentance process* began at that very hour and by *continuing in his word* she could avail herself of the Savior's offer of forgiveness.

As the woman walked away in the light of Christ, Jesus turned to the people and said, "I am the light of the world, he that followeth me shall not walk in darkness, but shall have the light of life" (John 8:12). "If ye believe not that I am he, ye shall die in your sins" (John 8:24). "When ye have lifted up the Son of man, then shall ye know that I am he" (John 8:28). Then said Jesus to those Jews who believed on him: "If ye continue in my word, then are ye my disciples indeed;

and ye shall know the truth, and the truth shall make you free" (John 8:31-32). Truth is the basis of the justice of God. The justice of God divides the wicked from the righteous. The brightness thereof is like the brightness of a flaming fire (1 Ne. 15:30).

The Flaming Sword of Truth
Turns Every Way to Keep the Way
of the Tree of Life

0, 1260 units

Diagram 14.3

Chapter 15

JESUS CHRIST AND HIM CRUCIFIED

> Paul wrote to the Corinthians: "And I, brethren, when I came to you, came not with excellency of speech or of wisdom, declaring unto you the testimony of God. For I determined not to know any thing among you, save Jesus Christ, and him crucified" (1 Cor. 2:1-2).

One of the great joys of life is to associate with those who have strong testimonies of Jesus Christ and esteem his works to be of great worth in their lives. Unfortunately, as Nephi once explained:

> "The things which some men esteem to be of great worth, both to the body and soul, others set at naught and trample under their feet. Yea, even the very God of Israel do men trample under their feet; I say, trample under their feet but I would speak in other words--they set him at naught, and hearken not to the voice of his counsels. And behold he cometh, according to the words of the angel in six hundred years from the time my father left Jerusalem. And the world, because of their iniquity, shall judge him to be a thing of naught; wherefore, they scourge him, and he suffereth it; and they smite him, and he suffereth it. Yea, they spit upon him, and he suffereth it, because of his loving kindness and his long-suffering towards the children of men."
> (1 Ne. 19:7-9.)

The Character of Jesus Christ

It is difficult to understand why any man would treat another person discourteously, but to treat the Son of God, the Creator of heaven and earth, with such contempt as described in scripture is almost incomprehensible. We might ask: "Did Jesus come to earth knowing he would receive this kind of insult and pain because he was a *weakling* as is so often depicted in the art of the world? Of course not! He was a manly man, stronger in character than any man who ever lived. He came here and suffered because of his loving kindness and his long-suffering towards the children of men.

The Pure Love of Christ

How can we comprehend such love? He was tempted in all points, yet he did not yield, and thus needed no rebuke or suffering for sin. Justice had no claim on him whatsoever. Yet so great was his love for us that he came here voluntarily knowing that he would suffer the kind of pain and abuse Nephi described, and even other pain incomprehensible to us that we might be redeemed from our sins.

We might ask ourselves, as the angel asked Nephi: "Knowest thou the condescension of God" (1 Ne. 11:16)? Do we know that the Lord God Omnipotent, who reigns in this universe, who was and is from all eternity to all eternity, came down from heaven to this very earth, among the children of men, and dwelt in a tabernacle of clay? Do we understand how in his coming to earth and suffering the pain of all men he descended below all things that he might comprehend all things, even the heights, and the depths, and the breadths of all existence, that he might raise every obedient soul unto exaltation (*Journal of Discourses*, 7:286; D&C 88:6)?

Trials
Many people have great cause for sorrow in this life because of trials, but he had a deeper sorrow than any mortal could experience. We might say: "Oh yes, but it was easier for him because he was the Son of God." But, in reality, it was infinitely harder. He took upon himself the sins of the world.

As King Benjamin foresaw: He suffered temptations, and pain of body, hunger, thirst, and fatigue, even more than man can suffer, except it be unto death; for behold, blood came from every pore, so great was his anguish for the wickedness and abominations of his people (Mosiah 3:7). He suffered temptations more than any man; he suffered hunger more than any man; he suffered thirst more than any man; he suffered fatigue more than any man. Because of his mortal nature, he suffered; because of his divine perfection, he endured, not easier but harder. He would walk day and night without food to reach an appointed destination so that he would be prepared for an important occasion. Jesus could have avoided the fatigue by using his divine power. Yet even at the moment of greatest fatigue, he never used his power inappropriately.

Jesus Christ—More Than a Great Teacher
He was called Jesus Christ, the Son of God, the Father of heaven and earth, the Creator of all things from the beginning; and his mother was called Mary. And he went forth among the children of men performing mighty miracles, such as healing the sick, raising the dead, causing the lame to walk, the deaf to hear, and the blind to see, and curing all manner of diseases.

And after all this, they considered him simply a man, and said he had a devil, and they scourged him, and crucified him. (Mosiah 3:5-6, 8-9.) And all this he allowed of his own free will and choice because of his loving kindness and long-suffering towards the children of men (1 Ne. 19:9).

Now, after all the mighty miracles which he performed, and after all the prophecies which were made of him were clearly fulfilled before the people, and remember, the people of those days knew those prophecies much better than we do today (2 Ne. 25:5), how could they have considered him simply a man? Even more absurd, how could anyone today call him simply a great teacher? How inconsistent can the world be? Is lying consistent with being a great teacher? If he had been simply a great teacher, why did he claim to be the Son of God, the long awaited Messiah? Great teachers do not lie! He was indeed a great teacher, the greatest of all teachers, but he was much, much more.

Jesus is the Christ
Jesus Christ was precisely who he said he was. He was the Son of God, and he suffered beyond anything that mortal man can comprehend as part of paying justice for the sins of all his creations, whenever or wherever those sins were, are, or will be committed. Why he had to suffer so, we are not told, but that he did so, none can deny. In a poem composed around the great vision of the degrees of glory, Joseph Smith made clear that the sacrifice of the Savior pertained to all Elohim's children:

"I beheld round the throne holy angels and hosts,
And sanctified beings from worlds that have been,
In holiness worshipping God and the Lamb,
For ever and ever. Amen and amen.

"And now after all of the proofs made of him,
By witnesses truly, by whom he was known,
This is mine, last of all, that he lives; yea, he lives!
And sits on the right hand of God on his throne.

"And I heard a great voice bearing record from heav'n,
He's the Saviour and only begotten of God;
By him, of him, and through him, the worlds were all
    made,
Even all that career in the heavens so broad.

"Whose inhabitants, too, from the first to the last,
Are sav'd by the very same Saviour of ours;
And, of course, are begotten God's daughters and sons
By the very same truths and the very same powers."
(*Millennial Star*, 4:51.)

Justice accepted Jesus' sacrifice from the moment he accepted the divine call from our Father in Heaven, long before the foundation of this world was laid, that all those who would believe in him and exercise faith in him could receive a remission of sins, even as though he had already suffered for sins, independent of the time frame relative to his actual sacrifice on this earth nearly two thousand years ago (Mosiah 3:13). In the words of Isaiah, the Father saw the travail of his soul and was satisfied (Is. 53:11).

No Substitutes for the Savior

Had Jesus failed to atone for our sins, would there

have been a substitute? No! There were no substitutes had Jesus failed in his atoning mission despite what is often said: "Oh, if Jesus had failed, the Father would have provided another and another until one would finally succeed in saving us." No! The very idea lessens the Savior. When we truly fathom that no substitutes were possible once Jehovah was called, we are led to honor and to praise and to reverence this dear brother of ours forever and ever. Indeed, there is no other name given whereby salvation can come.

Jesus Christ was fully committed to his atoning mission. Though the suffering would be so intense, the agony so deep, that even the Only Begotten Son of God, with all his power, would marvel at its intensity, and even allow thoughts of letting the Atonement pass unfulfilled enter his mind, yet, glory be to God, his unceasing desire to do the will of the Father prevailed, preeminent above all other feelings and desires.

Jesus Christ Is Our Exemplar
Though without sin Jesus showed us the way by being baptized. He said: "Follow thou me" (2 Ne. 31:10); "I have set an example for you" (3 Ne. 18:16). After his passion Jesus "showed himself alive" to the apostles and taught them for 40 days about the kingdom of God (Acts 1:3). They were commanded to tarry in Jerusalem until they had received the gift of the Holy Ghost (Acts. 1:4-5). It was *8 days* after the ascension that *3 x 1000* people were spiritually *reborn* by being baptized and receiving the gift of the *Holy Ghost*. This occurred "when the day of Pentecost was fully come," when "they were all with one accord in one place" (Acts 2:1, 41).

The day of Pentecost is the "feast of weeks," the 50th day after Passover, counting inclusively (BD, p. 673). In AD 34 this was Friday, 20 May, the 7 week anniversary of Passover (Friday, AD 1 April 33).

During our lifetimes we too will be tried even as Abraham to determine the level of our faith in the Lord Jesus Christ. Joseph Smith said:

> "We will have all kinds of trials to pass through. It is quite as necessary for us to be tried as it was for Abraham and other men of God. God will feel after you and he will take hold of you and wrench your very heart strings, and if you cannot stand it, you will not be fit for an inheritance in the Celestial Kingdom of God (JD 24:197).

At the point of our ultimate trial, may we follow the example of the Son in doing the will of the Father. As we seek with all our might, mind, and strength to follow his commandments, it is comforting to know that the Lord is pleading our cause before the Father, saying (D&C 45:3-5):

> "Father, behold the sufferings and death of him who did no sin, in whom thou wast well pleased; behold the blood of thy Son which was shed, the blood of him whom thou gavest that thyself might be glorified; Wherefore, Father, spare these my brethren that believe on my name, that they may come unto me and have everlasting life."

Let us ever live worthy of the divine mediation of our Lord and Savior, Jesus Christ, the Chief Cornerstone of the kingdom of God.

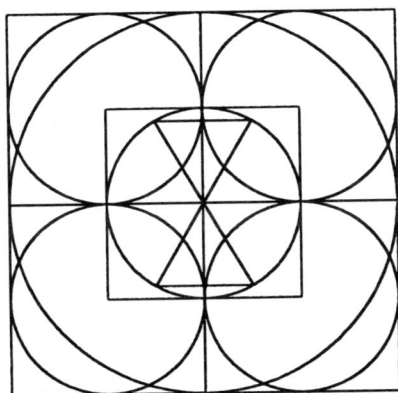

Scripture Index

131:1-4, p. 6
132:19, pp. 6, 17, 20, 25,
132:37, p. 6
133:5, 14, p. 7
133:10-13, p. 53
133:12-13, pp. 38, 101
133:12-15, pp. 62, 99
133:14-15, p. 103
135:1, pp. 53, 88
135:3, pp. 54, 91
136:1-2, p. 92
138:18, p. 13

Moses
1:4, pp, 17, 19
3:8-10, p. 19
3:16-17, p. 20
4:2, p. 35
4:3-4, p. 5
4:31, pp. 20, 49, 112
6:7, p. 85
6:48-63, p. 20
6:59, pp. 3, 13
6:60, pp. 8, 77
6:62, p. 19
7:26, pp. 5, 99
7:45-46, pp. 23, 35
7:56, 26 p. 13
7:60-64, p. 114
7:61-62, pp. 67, 103
7:64, p. 113
7:68, p. 107
8:1, p. 107

Abraham
2:8-9, p. 39
2:8-11, p. 8
2:11, pp. 4, 16, 17, 37
3:26, pp. 6, 40
4:1, 18, p. 4

Joseph Smith—Matthew
1:12-13, p. 22
1:13, pp. 92
1:26, 36, pp. 51, 113
1:31, p. 103
1:32, p. 105

Joseph Smith—History
1:3, pp. 39, 56
1:11-14, pp. 46-47
1:14-17, pp. 44, 55
1:17, pp. 47, 110
1:28-34, pp. 58-59
1:29, pp. 56, 62
1:33, pp. 56, 62
1:36, p. 55
1:41, p. 37
1:42, 59, p. 62
1:42, 51-54, pp. 63-64
1:59, pp. 54, 66
1:72, p. 71

Articles of Faith
1:4, pp. 20, 107
1:10, p. 50

Subject Index